SCHOOL IMPROVEMENT NETWORKS AND COLLABORATIVE INQUIRY

EMERALD PROFESSIONAL LEARNING NETWORK SERIES

In the current international policy environment, teachers are viewed as learning-oriented adaptive experts. Required to be able to teach increasingly diverse sets of learners, teachers must be competent in complex academic content, skilful in the craft of teaching and able to respond to fast changing economic and policy imperatives. The knowledge, skills and attitudes needed for this complex profession requires teachers to engage in collaborative and networked career-long learning. The types of learning networks emerging to meet this need comprise a variety of collaborative arrangements including inter-school engagement, as well as collaborations with learning partners, such as universities or policy-makers. More understanding is required, however, on how learning networks can deliver maximum benefit for both teachers and students.

Emerald Professional Learning Network Series aims to expand current understanding of professional learning networks and the impact of harnessing effective networked collaboration.

Published Titles:

Formalise, Prioritise and Mobilise: How School Leaders Secure the Benefits of Professional Learning Networks
Chris Brown and Jane Flood

School Improvement Networks and Collaborative Inquiry: Fostering Systemic Change in Challenging Contexts
Mauricio Pino Yancovic, Alvaro González Torres, Luis Ahumada Figueroa and Christopher Chapman

Forthcoming in the Series:

Professional Learning Networks: Facilitating Educational Transformation
Edited by Leyton Schnellert

Professional Learning Networks in Design-based Research Interventions
Stuart McNaughton and Mei Kuin Lai

SCHOOL IMPROVEMENT NETWORKS AND COLLABORATIVE INQUIRY

Fostering Systematic Change in Challenging Contexts

BY

MAURICIO PINO YANCOVIC
Pontificia Universidad Católica de Valparaíso, Chile

ALVARO GONZÁLEZ TORRES
Pontificia Universidad Católica de Valparaíso, Chile

LUIS AHUMADA FIGUEROA
Pontificia Universidad Católica de Valparaíso, Chile

AND

CHRISTOPHER CHAPMAN
University of Glasgow, UK

emerald
PUBLISHING

United Kingdom – North America – Japan – India
Malaysia – China

Emerald Publishing Limited
Howard House, Wagon Lane, Bingley BD16 1WA, UK

First edition 2020

Copyright © 2020 Mauricio Pino Yancovic, Alvaro González Torres,
Luis Ahumada Figueroa and Christopher Chapman

Published under exclusive licence

Reprints and permissions service
Contact: permissions@emeraldinsight.com

British Library Cataloguing in Publication Data
A catalogue record for this book is available from the British
Library

ISBN: 978-1-78769-738-6 (Print)
ISBN: 978-1-78769-735-5 (Online)
ISBN: 978-1-78769-737-9 (Epub)

Printed and bound by CPI Group (UK) Ltd, Croydon, CR0 4YY

ISOQAR certified
Management System,
awarded to Emerald
for adherence to
Environmental
standard
ISO 14001:2004.

Certificate Number 1985
ISO 14001

INVESTOR IN PEOPLE

We want to dedicate this book to all the school leaders that work hard for the education of their students. We also want to dedicate this book to the families of these leaders, and to our families, that support and allow us to concentrate our energy to promote the systemic improvement of education.

CONTENTS

LIST OF FIGURES, ACRONYMS AND TABLES

FIGURES

ACRONYMS

MINEDUC   →   Chilean Ministry of Education (in Spanish,
                Ministerio de Educación).
PLN   →   Professional Learning Network.
PME   →   Educational Improvement Plan (in Spanish,
                Plan de Mejoramiento Escolar).

SIMCE   →   System of Measurement of Educational
                Achievement (in Spanish, Sistema de
                Medición de la Calidad de la Educación).
SIN   →   School Improvement Network.
UNESCO   →   United Nations Educational, Scientific and
                Cultural Organization.

TABLES

ACKNOWLEDGEMENTS

We gratefully acknowledge the support from the Leadership Center for Educational Improvement, LIDERES EDUCA-TIVOS at Pontificia Universidad Católica de Valparaíso, and from the Ministry of Education of the Chilean Government (MINEDUC). In addition, funding from the PIA-CONICYT Basal Funds for Centers of Excellence Project FB0003 is gratefully acknowledged.

We are also grateful to United Nations Educational, Scientific and Cultural Organization (UNESCO) for supporting the "Study about the implementation of the School Improvement Networks" and to all the researchers who have participated in this study.

We would also like to thank all the researchers who have participated in the National Evaluation of the School Improvement Networks; Christopher Brown and Cindy Portman for their valuable feedback to improve the ideas, reflections and the general quality of this book; and Kimberley Chadwick for her detailed feedback and editorial suggestions.

ABOUT THE AUTHORS

Mauricio Pino Yancovic is a Researcher of the Leadership Center for Educational Improvement, LIDERES EDUCA-TIVOS. His academic and research experience is focused in educational policy, school networks and evaluation. He currently coordinates the national evaluation of the school improvement networks strategy in Chile, and leads programs to support collaborative inquiry networks. He completed his Ph.D. in Educational Policy Studies from the University of Illinois at Urbana Champaign. He has worked in teacher professional development programs and researched teachers transforming identity in the context of the Chilean teacher evaluation and incentives system. Recent publications include Study Abroad for Preservice Teachers: Critical Learning and Teaching in a Diverse Context (book chapter published by IGI Global, with Allison Witt, and Brandi Neal). A critique to the standardization for accountability: narrative of resistance of the assessment system in Chile (*Cadernos CEDES* journal, with Gonzálo Oyarzún and Ivan Salinas).

Alvaro González Torres is a Researcher of the Leadership Center for Educational Improvement, LIDERES EDUCA-TIVOS. His academic work centers on the interplay between practice and policy in the field of educational improvement and effectiveness, which was the subject of his doctoral thesis. He has been part of research and development projects on education policy and system reform, instructional systems, educational leadership and professional learning, from a comparative and critical perspective. He is currently coordinating programs associated with systemic leadership, collaborative school networks and the change in the governance model of public education in Chile. Recent publications include: The relationship between leadership preparation and the level of teachers' interest in assuming a principalship in Chile (School Leadership & Management journal, with Sergio Galdames); Comparing international curriculum systems: the international instructional systems study (The Curriculum journal, with Brian Creese and Tina Isaacs); Can Educational Technical Assistance (ATE) be a Strategy for Teacher Professional Development? Reflections from a Chilean Case Study (in Perspectiva Educacional journal); and Quality Assurance in Chile's Municipal Schools: Facing the Challenge of Assuring and Improving Quality in Low Performing Schools (book chapter published by InTech, with Luis Ahumada and Carmen Montecinos).

Luis Ahumada Figueroa is a Professor at the School of Psychology, and a Researcher at LIDERES EDUCATIVOS, Leadership Center for Educational Improvement. He is currently investigating Distributed Leadership in Schools serving high poverty and socially vulnerable communities. His most recent co-authored publications in refereed journals include: A goal orientation analysis of teachers' motivations to participate in the school self-assessment processes of a quality assurance system in Chile (Educational Assessment, Evaluation and Accountability, 2014); Understanding leadership in schools facing challenging circumstances: A Chilean case study (International Journal of Leadership in Education, 2015); Targets, threats and (dis)trust: The managerial troika for public school principals in Chile (Education Policy Analysis

Archives, 2015); Novice principals in Chile mobilizing change for the first time: Challenges and opportunities associated with a school's readiness for change (Educational Management Administration & Leadership, 2017).

Christopher Chapman is Chair of Educational Policy and Practice at the University of Glasgow in January 2013 and became the Founding Director of the Robert Owen Centre for Educational Change (ROC). Prior to this he was Professor of Education at the University of Manchester and previously held academic and research posts at the universities of Nottingham and Warwick. Before moving into academia Chris taught in challenging secondary schools in Birmingham where he undertook a part-time MA before completing his Ph.D. thesis on intervention and improvement in schools in challenging circumstances. He is the Director of Policy Scotland the University's Centre for public policy research and knowledge exchange and PI of Children's Neighbourhoods Scotland a major three-year Scottish Government investment in researching and developing a place-based approach to tackle poverty and improve outcomes for children and young people. He is also Co-Director of ESRC/Scottish Government funded What Works Scotland Centre and seconded part-time as Senior Academic Advisor to Scottish Government.

INTRODUCTION

Education decentralization has been a prominent feature of educational reforms across various nations, under the assumption that local problems require local solutions (McGinn & Welsh, 1999). However, in many countries, decentralization has been paradoxically accompanied by centralization in school governance and decision over curriculum and instruction, especially by the implementation of standardized accountability measures, which increase teacher and principal responsibilities and decrease their autonomy (Jeong & Luschei, 2018). Also, while some educational reforms that have relied on decentralization have had a positive impact in some schools, many others have struggled to develop the necessary capacity to improve (Wohlstetter, Malloy, Chau, & Polhemus, 2003). As a way to address this issue, researchers have highlighted networking as a good strategy to build teachers' and principals' capacities through collaboration between schools, promoting a systemic vision of educational improvement (Bryk, Gomez, & Grunow, 2010; Chapman, 2013; Muijs, 2010; Muijs, West, & Ainscow, 2010; Rincón-Gallardo & Fullan, 2016).

Chile joined this international trend by developing a set of ambitious reforms in the past five years, prompting a move toward a collaborative educational culture among schools. To bring this principle to practice, in 2015 the Chilean Ministry of Education (MINEDUC), through its General Education

Division, launched the School Improvement Network (SIN) strategy. More than 500 networks were created to support state-funded schools across all 15 regions of the country. These networks bring together an average of 10 schools, each represented by their principal and curriculum coordinator, in addition to a representative of the local education authority and a ministry supervisor. They meet monthly throughout the school year, which runs from March to December, with the purpose of generating and transferring good practices and analyzing improvement processes among school leaders (MINEDUC, 2016a).

The implementation of the SIN strategy represents a radical cultural change, since competition is a prominent feature of the Chilean school system due to its market-oriented principles. Since the 1980s, Chile, as many educational systems around the world (Apple, 2005; McCarthy, Pitton, Kim, & Monje, 2009; Rizvi & Lingard, 2010), has applied market-oriented principles to education policy using the discourse of quality assurance and accountability to argue that competition would drive educational improvement (Ahumada, Montecinos, & González, 2012; Falabella, 2016). The marketization and privatization of education challenges the values of collaboration, trust and collective learning that school networks promote as paths for change and improvement. Far from promoting sustainable and positive changes, market-oriented educational policies have been associated with an increase of public school closings, escalating the gentrification and segregation of education and cities, harming traditionally marginalized minority groups (Lipman, 2011; McCarthy & Sanya, 2014; Núñez, Soto, & Solís, 2013; Pino-Yancovic, 2015). This global scenario makes the case of Chile even more interesting to study because it maintains and promotes contradictory policies for the same declared goal: improve the quality of education. Fundamentally, at stake is the understanding of what educational improvement means and entails. While high-stakes individual accountability policies attribute educational progress to each individual school, the logic of school networks relies on educational improvement as a systemic task (González, Pino, & Ahumada, 2017).

PROFESSIONAL LEARNING NETWORKS

The SINs resemble what the literature identifies as Professional Learning Networks (PLNs). PLNs are composed by a group of professionals who engage in collaborative learning processes with others, outside of their everyday community of practice, with the general goal to improve teaching and learning in their own schools (Brown & Poortman, 2018). In fact, certain conditions associated with the effectiveness of PLNs are relevant for SINs: *purpose*, *collaboration* and *inquiry*.

One of the most recurrent recommendation for effective PLNs is that they should have a clear, shared and specific *purpose* (Chapman et al., 2016a; Hubers & Poortman, 2018; Leithwood, 2018, Leithwood & Azah, 2016; Muijs et al., 2010; Rincón-Gallardo & Fullan, 2016; Poortman & Brown, 2018). In competitive contexts, such as the Chilean one, Armstrong and Ainscow (2018) argue that network purposes should specify the particular benefits that the networks will add to each member and their educational institution, a condition that Brown and Poortman (2018) relate to explicit and meaningful individual and group learning goals.

Collaboration is another condition for effective PLNs. The essence of networks is that two or more participants interact and share knowledge and resources (Chapman, 2015; Katz & Earl, 2010; Muijs et al., 2010). Collaboration requires an honest commitment to share and work together among different people and an involvement of these people with the purpose for which they are collaborating (Duffy & Gallagher, 2016; Muijs et al., 2010).

Finally, the literature highlights collaborative *inquiry* as methodology of work that allows participants to collect, analyze and monitor the activities of the network (Ainscow, Dyson, Goldrick, & West, 2016; Chapman et al., 2016a; DeLuca, Shulha, Luhanga, Shulha, Christou, & Klinger, 2015; Poortman & Brown, 2018). Collaborative inquiry is carried out through a cyclical process (DeLuca et al., 2015; Pino, González, & Ahumada, 2018). This methodological approach to PLNs also involves what Hubers and Poortman (2018) refer to as *reflective professional inquiry*, where participants in the PLN "discuss their underlying belief about teaching; share and clarify their pedagogical motives; collectively question ineffective teaching routines; and find proactive ways to acknowledge and respond to differences and conflict" (p. 199).

The central tenant of PLNs is that, by an active participation in their networks, all members of the PLN will benefit from a collective learning process. School leaders will be able to apply the knowledge generated within their networks back in their own schools, and the ultimate goal of this process is improving students' learning. In this regard, it is relevant to highlight that PLNs can serve multiple student learning goals, not only what is measured by standardized tests. For instance, students' learning can also address "children's physical and mental well-being and their fortitude, as well as more instrumental notions such as children's learning and academic performance" (Brown & Flood, 2019, p. 8).

To mobilize knowledge among networks and schools, PLNs are composed by *brokers*, network members who occupy key structural positions to link networks with their own institution. They are responsible to connect, share and mobilize knowledge between networks, schools and other relevant institutions in their immediate context, crossing the borders between and within their own community of practice (Poortman & Brown, 2018).

Brown and Flood (2019) identify three main courses of action that school leaders can perform to brokerage the PLN knowledge once they are back in their schools: (1) keep participating staff on track: leaders ensure that the PLN projects remain a priority in the hearts and minds of staff and teachers; (2) making the PLN purposeful: support and remind school staff that the PLN projects and activities are not additional tasks for the school, rather they are part of their current functions, making sure that staff is aware of the importance and potential impact of PLNs; and (3) formalize PLN action as a priority in linking the PLN activities with their own school improvement plan, staff hours, school goals and strategies.

The effort and dedication to support effective school networks and PLNs indicates that is beneficial for principals, teachers and students. There is strong evidence that school networks promote principals' leadership capacities and improve teachers' practices (Chapman et al., 2015, 2016a; Leithwood & Azah, 2016). Some studies also indicate that schools that participate in effective school networks improve students' outcomes (Chapman & Muijs, 2013; Hadfield & Chapman, 2009). The literature also emphasizes that school networks provide the opportunity to achieve cost-effective educational innovations (Munby & Fullan, 2016). In addition, studies on PLNs highlight that they can mobilize a wide range of research knowledge allowing to improve educational practices of schools that compose the network (Brown & Flood, 2019). Finally, the development of school networks as regional or national strategies, support bottom-up policies that can better articulate a diversity of demands of communities, school leaders and teachers (Azorín & Muijs, 2017).

Despite these benefits, evidence also stresses that ineffective networks could lead to unintended consequences and be harmful for educational systems (Rincón-Gallardo & Fullan, 2016). For instance, network participants can engage in interorganizational struggles, which could lead to losing sight of the public objectives that networks should be serving. Also, networks can engage in *groupthink*, being self-protective about mainstream group ideas and solutions to problems (Ehren & Perryman, 2018; Mayne & Rieper, 2003). Centralized networks can also incite resistance from their participants, especially when they function in a hierarchical manner, forcing diverse actors to apply and replicate specific strategies, instead of promoting learning based on collaboration and horizontality (Greany & Ehren, 2016). Additionally, external factors, such as a market-oriented and competitive environment, can inhibit collaborative practices and generate distrust among participants of networks, especially when they do not perceive direct benefits of participating in these types of collaborative arrangements (Armstrong & Ainscow, 2018). Finally, studies about PLNs in contexts of accountability and high-stakes testing pressure professionals obstructing their possibilities to reflect about data analysis to implement new practices (Godfrey, 2017, in Poortman & Brown, 2018).

BOOK GUIDING QUESTIONS

All the unintended consequences mentioned above justify the relevance of studying how policies that promote networks of schools are developed, and how they operate within a context that constrains and hinders collaboration. There are not many studies that follow the design and implementation of school networks as they occur (Hargreaves & Fullan, 2012), and Chile offers a unique opportunity to research in detail how the SINs have been developed and enacted. Most of the literature on networks in education looks at experiences in Europe and North America (Rincón-Gallardo & Fullan, 2016), with fewer evidence from education systems in the Global South, such as Chile. Additionally, for the past 40 years, competition among schools for pupil enrollment has been the main driver of educational improvement in Chile (Carrasco & Fromm, 2016; Verger, Bonal, & Zancajo, 2016). Although schools are now expected to work in networks, they are held to account individually through high-stakes standardized testing and external inspections, then, there are reasonable uncertainties for SINs to be able to support the development of collaborative practices and mobilize knowledge between schools.

The National Education Quality Assurance Agency creates an annual classification scheme, based mostly in the System of Measurement of Educational Achievement (in Spanish Sistema de Medición de la Calidad de la Educación, SIMCE), where schools are individually categorized with a high, medium, medium-low or insufficient performance. Schools that are classified as insufficient for four years can be closed by the Ministry of Education, which makes them face extreme challenging internal and external circumstances and a great deal of pressure to improve (Pino-Yancovic, Salinas, & Oyarzún, 2016).

The clash of opposite values, reflected in specific educational policies, is examined in this book by researching empirical data about the design and implementation of the SIN strategy at a national scale. Specifically, this book analyzes the collaborative practices that principals and curriculum coordinators perceive in their networks and how the knowledge that is shared and produced within networks can (or cannot) be useful to respond to challenges that school leaders face in the daily life of their own schools. Specifically, three main questions guide the research presented in this book:

(1) What kind of knowledge is mobilized within SINs and among the schools that compose them?

(2) What types of collaborative practices among school leaders are promoted by the SINs?

(3) What are the challenges and possibilities for the development of sustainable school networks in a market-oriented educational context?

To answer these questions, from a mixed-methods perspective (Greene, 2007), we analyze the practices that occur within SINs employing collaborative inquiry as a framework, based on the theoretical review of DeLuca et al. (2015). Specifically, collaborative inquiry constitutes the substantive theory to mix the findings of two independent studies about the SIN policy. The primary research is a multi-site case study conducted in 2016 to characterize the process and value of collaborative practices of 15 SINs from different regions of the country. The supplementary research is a national study of SINs functioning from the perspective of principals and curriculum coordinators, based on data from an online questionnaire answered by 398 of the 483 existing networks in 2017. This research provides evidence of the depth and spread of the knowledge and practices that participants from these networks state that they make use of in their own schools.

The findings of this mixed-methods study highlight both challenges and opportunities for SIN to be sustainable as a national strategy for systemic improvement, within a particularly challenging context for fostering collaboration. In general, SINs are highly valued as a significant strategy to exchange pedagogical practices and professional experiences, reducing the isolation that traditionally school leaders have faced in Chile and building professional capital. However, participants have faced many difficulties to connect their work within SINs with their school practices. Linking with the literature on PLNs, we discuss the findings of this study around the issue of network sustainability, stressing the importance of network leadership and conditions of system infrastructure to mobilize network knowledge and practices to schools, increasing the potential impact of this knowledge in transforming schools' practices, and the process of network members becoming active agents of their own networks.

BOOK CHAPTERS

This book is divided into five chapters. Chapter 1, "School Improvement Networks in a Market-oriented Educational Context," describes the rationale and implementation of the SIN strategy in Chile. Here we address the policy-level contradiction, where schools are expected to collaborate in networks while being accountable individually through high-stakes testing and external inspections.

Chapter 2, "Collaborative Inquiry in Challenging Contexts," outlines the rationale underpinning the importance of school networks to enable and foster collaboration, and the distribution of practices and knowledge among schools, enhancing their capacity for improvement through an interconnected approach. Specifically, we address the relevance of better defining and understanding the idea of *promoting a culture of collaboration* in education and also the value of using collaborative inquiry as a methodological framework to analyze SINs' organization and practices.

In Chapter 3, "A National Mixed-methods Study of School Networks in Chile," we describe the foundations of the methodological approach of this book, based on Jennifer Greene's (2007) description of mixed-methods research as a way of thinking with the overall purpose of better understanding social phenomena. This chapter also describes the mixed-methods rationale and design, and presents thick description of the methods and participants of both studies: the multi-site case study of the 15 SINs in five regions of Chile and the national questionnaire of principals and curriculum coordinators from 398 SINs.

Chapter 4, "School Networks: From Competition to Collaboration," describes and analyzes the findings from the mixed-methods research. Findings are organized and presented using three core features of collaborative inquiry: (1) Identification of common challenges: SINs focus on the dissemination and analysis of national policies relevant for schools, the development or implementation of key national policy instruments and on the development of professional capacities by sharing educational experiences. But also, participants from some networks have not yet defined a clear purpose for their network, besides being part of informative meetings. (2) Inquiry and taking action: some SINs address formal contents and skills that school leaders should analyze in order to enhance the quality of their Educational Improvement Plans (PMEs). In other SINs, participants share successful or innovative experiences and projects and collectively analyze pedagogical projects included in schools' PME. Principals and curriculum coordinators also identify and replicate actions developed in the networks into their schools. (3) Monitoring and reflection: this is the less-developed area of networks in Chile, and network members demand more opportunities to provide feedback about the impact of networks activities in the schools. In general, networks are responding to significant challenges that school leaders are facing; they value the knowledge of networks and use this knowledge in their own schools. At this stage, networks have been able to support the development for professional capital of the network's members, and most of the network are dedicated to share experiences and projects, less in developing joint actions or projects.

The fifth and final chapter of this book, "Sustainability of the School Improvement Networks," is dedicated to describe the development of conditions for effective PLN to support the professional capital among school leaders, as a result of the SIN strategy. To allow SIN becoming a sustainable strategy, this chapter emphasizes the relevance of leadership capacities for *leading downwards*, *lateral leadership* and *leading upwards*, mobilizing influence and power relations within, between and beyond networks. Finally, there is a reflection about the role of systemic leaders to actively shape the *system infrastructure*, and its relevance for SINs to become a meaningful policy, able to change cultural patterns beyond the remit of networks themselves.

The fundamental question asked by our book is whether it is possible to move school leaders from a culture of competition to a culture of collaboration using school networks to promote systemic improvement and, at the same time, maintaining a high number of market-oriented educational policies. Our answer is that it is not only possible but desirable from the perspective of school leaders to move forward along a path of collective networked learning. The barriers to the sustainability of school networks in Chile are technical and political; from this context, it is possible to argue that countries that seek to implement PLNs as a national policy should be precise about the capabilities that leaders require, reshape the idea of accountability and support the capacities of network members for *leading downwards*, *lateral leadership* and *leading upwards*. Far from being just a technical problem, and how knowledge can be better mobilized, it also involves addressing how relations of power should be mobilized among principals, curriculum coordinators and ministry supervisors to better define the expected role for school leaders to shape the educational system that we all need.

1

SCHOOL IMPROVEMENT NETWORKS IN A MARKET-ORIENTED EDUCATIONAL CONTEXT

International evidence shows that numerous educational systems have opted for school networks to support the improvement not only of those schools in difficulty but also the system as a whole (Azorín & Muijs, 2017; Chapman, 2015; Feys & Devos, 2015; Rincón-Gallardo & Fullan, 2016). In the global north, these network initiatives are supported by methodologies of data gathering and analysis to improve practices, involving many schools, teachers and/or school leaders. Many school networks with different purposes where developed in the 1990s to address diverse educational challenges (Hadfield & Chapman, 2009). Some of these experiences focused on supporting good professional relationships among teachers, while others used networks for professional from different schools, not only teachers, to address similar educational challenges (Bryk et al., 2010; Lieberman & Grolnick, 1996; Little, 1993; Wohlstetter, Malloy, Chau, & Polhemus, 2003).

Current examples of school networks have focused their endeavor in supporting the professional capacities of principals and teachers to inquiry and enhance student learning. In Scotland, Chapman et al. (2016b) studied the School Improvement Partnership Programme (SIPP), a three-year collaborative and inquiry-driven initiative of eight networks distributed in 14 districts supported by the Robert Owen Center for Educational Change, which was designed to improve educational experiences and outcomes of children from disadvantaged backgrounds and thus contribute to closing the attainment gap in Scotland. Also, Brown and Flood (2019) describe and analyze the experience of Research Learning Networks (RLN) in England, focused in generating research-informed practices in a series of workshop with 14 networks, comprising 110 staff from 55 schools.

There are also examples of similar networks in Australia, Austria, Belgium and Spain, many of them including data gathering and analysis to improve teachers practices and support the development of leadership capacities of principals, curriculum coordinators and teachers (Azorín & Muijs, 2017; Feys & Devos, 2015; Matthews, Moorman, & Nusche 2008; Stoll, Moorman, & Rahm, 2008). Broadly, all of these networking initiatives can be described as Professional Learning Networks (PLNs).

In contrast, fewer examples of these networks can be found in Latin America, although those that do exist offer interesting insights. For instance, there are networking initiatives similar to PLNs, such as the Learning Community Project in Mexico and Escuela Nueva in Colombia. These examples share the fact that both have evolved from previous grassroots movements into official national programs. Their focus is on empowering students to guide their own learning, supporting innovative pedagogical practices between teachers and students, nurturing horizontal relationship of dialogue, co-learning and mutual influence between students, teachers and leaders (Rincón-Gallardo, 2019).

The case of Chile offers a very different picture, as it is possible to find network initiatives dating back over 30 years. A well-known example is MECE RURAL, a national program focused on improving rural education by creating networks called "Microcentros Rurales" (rural micro-centers), which bring together teachers from several small rural schools. This program has been running since 1992, and it aims to improve teachers' practices and support collaborative professional relations (Avalos, 1999; Moreno, 2007). Similarly, municipal departments of education have traditionally formed and supported thematic networks among public municipal schools focused on Early Childhood Education, English as a Second Language, Spanish Language and Mathematics (Fuentealba & Galaz, 2008). Also, some networks specifically focus on the professional development of teachers, such as the Teachers of Teachers Network (Montecinos, Pino, Campos, Domínguez, & Carreño, 2014), and others that connect teachers with university academics, such as the network for the transformation and improvement of science education (González-Weil, Cortéz, Pérez, Bravo, & Ibaceta, 2013).

More recently, networking has been positioned as one of the core principles of a significant reform to the public education system in Chile. This reform, represented by Law No. 21.040, changes the governance structure for the provision of public education in Chile. Starting in 2018, municipal schools began to be transferred to the first four Local Public Education Services, and this process will continue over a period of 10 years (Bellei, 2018). By 2028, the 345 municipal departments of education should be reorganized into 70 Local Public Education Services, which will operate as networks to guarantee access to quality education with equity in their territory.

In addition to these public initiatives, there are several experiences led by private-subsidized foundations running state-funded schools that have developed networking as a way to efficiently administrate resources, implement educational programs and promote innovation. Some well-known examples are *Belén Educa* foundation with 12 schools and 18 years of existence, the *Sociedad de Instrucción Primaria* that has been organized as a network since 2001 with 19 schools, the Network of Leading Schools sponsored by *Fundación Chile* since 2007 with 110 schools, the *Fundación Oportunidad* working with 28 early years' centers since 2007 applying the A Good Start program, and the *Red La Salle Chile* operating with seven schools as a network since the 1980s (DEP, 2018).

Among these experiences, the most recent school network initiative is the School Improvement Network (SIN) strategy, which was launched nationwide in 2015. That year, nearly 500 networks across all 15 regions of the country were created to support the improvement of municipal schools and, in some cases, private-subsidized schools.

The long tradition of school networks, the new administration of public education by the creation of the Local Public Education Services, the private-subsidized foundation projects and the nationwide SIN strategy reflect the significance of school networks for Chile. Nevertheless, there is scarce research about how networks function and even less evidence about the conditions to successfully operate in a market-oriented educational system.

A REFORM TO STRENGHTEN PUBLIC EDUCATION IN A MARKET-ORIENTED SYSTEM

Chile has been characterized as one of the first countries in the world to implement a set of neoliberal policies. Called the "neoliberal experiment", the military dictatorship of Augusto Pinochet (1973–1989) began to impose these policies, which were subsequently developed and updated by a center-left coalition of parties, during the democratic governments (1990–2010) (Bellei, 2015; Harvey, 2007; OECD, 2004; Taylor, 2006). This neoliberal perspective proposes that the organization and the management of education systems follow the same logic of markets. Schools must compete for students, and if this service is not of quality, then they will lose their customers and close (Peirano & Vargas, 2005). Lubienski and Lubienski (2014) point out that those who support the market as a way of organizing public education do so with the promise of increased effectiveness and efficiency to establish a direct link with consumers, who will choose the best education for their children, without having to go through bureaucrats or education experts that intervene with the power of their own decisions.

Two key educational policies reflect the market-oriented model of the Chilean educational system. First, a voucher system based on student enrollment and attendance to finance the educational system; if schools have low enrollment, then the administrator of that school has less resources to support the education that they provide. Second, a national standard-ized test (SIMCE) for high-stakes accountability purposes. These policies are connected and together foster a business capital model (Shirley, 2016). The idea is that schools will compete against each other to secure students' enrollment in order to have the necessary resources to enable them to subsist, while SIMCE results are expected to inform families' choice of schools for their children (Bellei & Vanni, 2015; Pino-Yancovic, 2015).

In addition, during the dictatorship, the administration of public primary and secondary schools was transferred to municipalities and private entities who received state funding through the voucher system. Until this day, municipalities run public schools through municipal departments of educational administration and are legally represented by the mayor of the municipality (Peirano & Vargas, 2005). Alternatively, some municipalities chose to devolve the administration of schools to a municipal corporation, but due to the high cost of this alternative, most municipalities opted for creating departments of educational administration (Taylor, 2006). As for private entities, they included individuals, companies and/or corporations, either for-profit or non-profit, who were authorized by the Ministry of Education to administer and run one or several schools. For two decades, private-subsidized schools could charge tuition to parents in addition to the state funds received through the voucher.

These policies have had negative consequences for the quality and equity in the education system (Valenzuela, Bellei, & De los Ríos, 2014), which led to massive social discontent demanding radical change (Bellei & Cabalin, 2013). As mentioned before, between 2014 and 2017, Chile started a process of comprehensive reform that has progressively transformed some of these policies from the dictatorship era (Valenzuela & Montecinos, 2017). One of the most important changes was the Inclusion Law, a policy that regulates school admissions, aimed to allow parents to choose and access educational institutions regardless of their economic capacity and to prevent publicly funded schools from profit seeking. Additionally, the law that creates a New System of Public Education, which changes the governance of public education by effectively replacing the municipal administration of schools with 70 Local Public Education Services. The declared objective of this set of reforms was to ensure education as a social right, and that public education becomes accessible to every child and young person, where all students will be able to

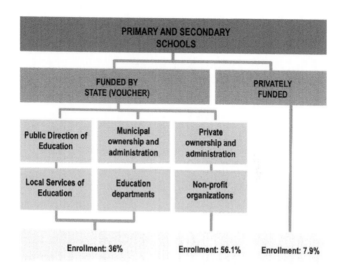

Fig. 1. Administration and Enrollment Share of Chilean Educational System.

experience an integral quality learning process. Despite this explicit support for public education, some key elements of the market-oriented model of education, that might be more difficult to change, such as the voucher based on pupil attendance and the high-stakes accountability system, were not included in the reform. Fig. 1 represents the administration and enrollment share of the Chilean educational system in this reform and transition period.

CHILE'S EDUCATIONAL IMPROVEMENT POLICY FRAMEWORK

Educational improvement is currently framed by various legal and policy instruments. One very relevant is the Law No. 20.501 that created the Preferential School Subsidy. This law provides additional resources to schools with a high proportion of students from low-income families and different levels of autonomy. Schools can use those resources to define and implement their own improvement strategies, contingent to their performance. As a result, the Preferential School Subsidy formally introduced for the first time a system of rewards and sanctions based on schools' performance measured by pupils' attainment in the national standardized test, SIMCE, and especially those students considered socially disadvantaged (Valenzuela & Montecinos, 2017).

Another very important policy is the National System for the Quality Assurance of Education, defined by the Law No. 20.529. This new system reorganized the role of the Ministry of Education and the National Council of Education and created two new institutions to assess, guide and support the performance of individual schools: The Education Quality Agency and the Superintendence of Education. Fig. 2 represents the current organization of this system.

The Quality Agency has been instrumental in maintaining and strengthening the high-stakes individual accountability system in Chile, as it is in charge of evaluating schools' performance based on their pupils' outcomes in SIMCE. This performance evaluation results in the sorting and classification of schools in four levels: high, medium, medium-low, or insufficient. Schools that are classified as insufficient receive an inspection visit to evaluate their pedagogical and management processes and receive guidance and support from the Quality Agency and the Ministry of Education; however, the law establishes that if these schools are classified as insufficient for four consecutive years, they can be closed by the Ministry of Education, facing very challenging internal and external circumstances (Bellei & Vanni, 2015).

This legal and policy framework indicates that schools are responsible for leading their improvement process through the design and implementation of an Educational Improvement

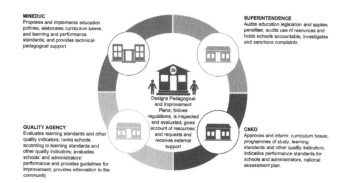

Fig. 2.   National System for the Quality Assurance of Education.
Source: **Adaptation and Translation Public Document National Council of Education (CNED).**

Plan (PME). According to the Ministry of Education, the PME is a tool "to guide, plan and materialize processes of institutional and pedagogical improvement of each educational community and for the integral development of its students" (MINEDUC, 2017b). PMEs are central component to promote institutional and pedagogical practices of schools and, with it, their outcomes (Román, 2008). To design and implement their PME, schools can request technical-pedagogical support from ministry supervisors, deployed in Provincial Departments of Education (DEPROV) and coordinated centrally by the General Education Division of the Ministry. Alternatively, schools can also use the resources obtained through special educational provision to hire Educational Technical Assistance entities, duly accredited in a Public Registry.

SCHOOL IMPROVEMENT NETWORKS

In the context of the comprehensive reform of public education, in 2014, the Ministry of Education focused the work of supervisors to support the development of capacities of school leaders, specifically to design and implement the PME. For that purpose, two supervision strategies were implemented: Direct School Visits and the School Improvement Networks. The direct visit focuses mainly in providing support for schools classified as insufficient by the Quality Agency, while the SIN has remained as a broad strategy to support all state-funded schools.

SIN started to be implemented in 2015 with 523 networks, involving over 5,500 schools in the country, with an average of seven network meetings during the school year (March–December), each lasting approximately five hours (MINEDUC, 2016a). In 2016 and 2017, the number of networks decreased to 505 and 483, respectively, but they maintained the average number and duration of meetings. Most SINs bring together between five and 15 schools, each represented by their principal and curriculum coordinator, in addition to a representative of the local administrator (often, a professional from the municipality) and one or two ministry supervisors. In 2018, a new government took office and changes were introduced in the Ministry of Education's agenda. Nevertheless, during 2018 and 2019, SIN has remained as an official support strategy of the Ministry of Education for state-funded schools, although with less resources available to sustain the strategy.

Despite recent changes, SIN purpose continues to be supporting and promoting a culture of collaboration among all members of the network, considering two dimensions: first, "to generate a new relationship between MINEDUC and schools based on mutual collaboration" and, second, "to generate opportunities for principals and curriculum coordinators to share experiences and for school and intermediate leaders to engage in professional development" (MINEDUC, 2016a, p. 9). Therefore, it was expected that SIN would develop professional capacity and learning with the aim of promoting and improving local education systems represented by each of the agents participating in the networks: school leaders, local education authorities and Ministry supervisors (MINEDUC, 2016a; 2016b). Consequently, SIN represents a systemic approach to the educational policy and a collaborative relationship between different levels of the school system, especially between the schools and the Ministry of Education.

According to MINEDUC (2017a), the focus and specific themes that SINs decided to work on changed and differed in each network. Among the main topics were the following: leadership practices, curricular management, pedagogical management, educational inclusion, diversity, frameworks of educational quality, new educational legislation and reform, educational evaluation, interculturality and resource management. The specific content of these topics should be informed by the pedagogical goals of each school member; thus, it is expected that principals and curriculum coordinators contribute with their own theoretical and practical knowledge to be shared and analyzed during network meetings. In addition, the ideal is that networks would be able to produce new knowledge to address the challenges that network members face in their own contexts (MINEDUC, 2017a). To ensure that these conditions are met, the Ministry defined three principles to guide the work of SIN at a national scale:

- *Purpose*: Defined as the shared goals that participants have to develop, for the general and final aim of improving student learning, leading networks to always consider the instructional core to define their purpose.

- *Collaboration*: The knowledge of network members must be socialized in order to support the capacity building of all those who participate in the network. Networks are required to value and use the knowledge of its participants.

• *Scope*: Networks should produce new knowledge that should be translated into new actions and practices.

The governance of each SIN is often taken up by a coordination team, formed by at least two school participants (principal or curriculum coordinator), one representative of the local educational administration and at least one Ministry supervisor. The coordination team plans and facilitates network meetings and activities. In addition, guidelines from MINEDUC indicate that supervisors have to adopt certain roles to support and mobilize the work of the networks, depending on the characteristic and activities of each one (MINEDUC, 2016): first, they can adopt a facilitator role to support the development of technical and pedagogical capacities of network members. Second, they can adopt an advisory role to guide and orient the reflection of network members around themes and processes of improvement, safeguarding a systemic analysis of topics related with their PME. And third, they can adopt a mediator role, ensuring the development of protocols that will allow the brokering of knowledge and learning from the networks to the school members.

The idea is that in SINs, school leaders will be able to not only share practices and knowledge and then implement these practices in their own school but also use the practical and theoretical knowledge of the network members to learn and create new understanding and solutions to educational challenges. School leaders should act as brokers, mobilizing the knowledge between the networks and their own schools. In addition to the roles of the principals and curriculum coordinators, SIN incorporates a representative of the local education administrator of schools, who is in charge of managing the time and recourses of the schools, and a supervisor of the Ministry of Education, who has to link the schools with national policies and guide the implementation of the school improvement plans. This diversity of members not only poses significant micropolitical nuisances to the networks but also becomes a concrete opportunity to promote systemic improvement because all relevant stakeholders, at different levels of the system, who can actually provide the support for change, are considered as active members of the network.

In a context of a national educational reform, the rationale of the MINEDUC for the development of SIN can be summarized as an attempt to increase the collaboration among schools and also change the relationship between schools and the Ministry of Education, supporting the professional development of school leaders who will share knowledge and practices in the networks. Fig. 3 represents MINEDUC's rationale for the development of SIN to support the development of professional capacities and a culture of collaboration.

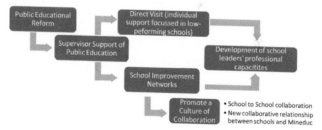

Fig. 3.   MINEDUC Rationale for Supporting the Development of SINs.

2

COLLABORATIVE INQUIRY IN CHALLENGING CONTEXTS

The Chilean Ministry of Education has promoted the SIN strategy with the purpose of mobilizing collaborative practices between schools and forging a new relationship of collaboration between ministry supervisors and schools. In 2016, Ministry guidelines for SIN identified three general stages of development for these networks, starting with an *implementation* stage focused on the exchange of practices; then it was expected that they would progress to a *community of practice* focused on addressing internal school process through joint actions among network members; and finally, they would reach a *professional learning community* stage focused on creating new knowledge for educational improvement and social transformations in their own context, meaning that different schools from a similar territory will be able to build a professional community and use this knowledge to address challenges that they are facing in their own schools. MINEDUC guidelines seem to be using the idea of *professional learning communities* and applying it to school networks, without an explicit and rigorous theoretical background about networking or school-to-school collaboration.

After two years of implementation, and building upon internal reviews and studies about the SIN strategy, the ministry's General Education Division produced a more precise and explicit objective for SIN and developed an intense short training program for supervisors, in order to better guide their work supporting these networks. The 2017 updated SIN general objective is:

> To develop a collaborative working culture among schools that are members of the school improvement network, with the purpose of generating individual and collective learning for networked improvement, and also for the improvement of the local communities where the network is embedded. (MINEDUC, 2017a, n/p)

To achieve this goal, the new guidelines from the General Education Division established several different strategic lines of action: (a) promoting the exchange of pedagogical and management practices; (b) focus the role of supervisors to generate and conduct networked improvement processes; (c) strengthen the organizational and technical structure of networks; (d) support local work; and (e) support the development of capacity for school improvement. These guidelines encourage supervisors to systematize the work, practices and knowledge of the network and provide feedback concerning what knowledge is generated and how it is distributed among network members, emphasizing that participants of the networks should share successful and unsuccessful practices, being both good opportunities for collective learning.

Regarding the structure of networks, SIN guidelines mandate supervisors to ensure that networks select their own coordinators. These can be a participant of the network, such as principal, curriculum coordinators or representatives of the local administrator, discouraging supervisors to occupy that position. Guidelines also suggest that part of the network activity should be the identification of resources, limitations and opportunities of the local context, especially social services (e.g., health services, youth centers and local neighbored boards), in order to make use of them for improvement purposes and also to respond more effectively to local challenges. Finally, these guidelines emphasize that networks should develop the capacities of school leaders to improve their own educational practices, from a systemic perspective, and that supervisors should contribute to, rather than dictate, the action plan of each network.

The strategic lines of action proposed by the Ministry for SIN cover many conditions that can support the development of effective Professional Learning Networks (PLNs), such as providing a suitable governance structure and appropriate working processes focused in promoting collaboration and procuring individual and collective learning opportunities (Brown & Poortman, 2018). Additionally, Ministry guidelines introduce an interesting approach to the local communities and specific context of each network, which resembles experiences in other countries where communities are involved in school networks, generating significant contributions for the learning and well-being of the students and their families (Chapman et al., 2016a; Rincón-Gallardo & Fullan, 2016). Finally, the SIN strategy is supported by the idea that meaningful and effective collaboration is a crucial component of leadership and teacher professional development (Chapman et al., 2015; Leithwood, 2018). As relevant as it is to have ambitious goals and strategic lines of action, to be properly implemented, these expected actions require professional capacity from the supervisor and school leaders for networks to become spaces of professional learning where knowledge is mobilized.

As it has been repeatedly established in the literature, when new reforms, such as the development of school networks, do not expand with a detailed proposal of capacity building for those implementing such reforms, they can be reduced to new mandates that school leaders could disregard as a new panacea that does not meet with their actual needs and challenges. In these cases, reforms can backfire, harming the educational system by using the reduced and valuable time of principals in activities that do not directly benefit them or their own schools (Hargreaves & Fullan, 2012; Rincón-Gallardo & Fullan, 2016). Most importantly, as it has been argued before, the values and principles of this policy are contradictory with other policies that are implemented at the same time, such as a high-stakes accountability and a market-oriented education system that promotes competition. As Hargreaves and Fullan (2012) have highlighted,

> *a big difference between successful systems and unsuccessful ones is that the former have a clear sense of direction and a high degree of coherence, and an interconnected set of policies and strategies as well as an embedded culture of improvement that provides that direction and coherence. (p. 175)*

COLLABORATIVE EDUCATIONAL CULTURE

The SIN strategy offers an interesting narrative about promoting a culture of collaboration among schools, but as evidence has clearly shown, collaboration is complex, and it has many nuances (Duffy & Gallagher, 2016; Hargreaves & Fullan, 2012; Katz & Earl, 2010). What might facilitate the understanding of what is *promoting a culture of collaboration* is to clarify that it is not a black or white endeavor, but it has many gray areas, and it is much more complex that the presence or absence of sharing professional practices, both at a school level and a network level.

At the school level, Hargreaves and Fullan (2012) draw on Hargreaves' previous work (Hargreaves, 1994) to describe how the good intention of promoting collaboration among professionals can be actually used to control them or to impose hierarchical policies that do not articulate with what teachers need to improve their own practices. These authors describe different professional cultures, one being individualism and then different categories of collaborative cultures: Balkanization, Contrived Collegiality and Professional Learning Communities. This categorization of collaborative cultures means that collaboration is not unique or pristine, but that schools can have different process, practices and establish different relationships among their professionals, even when they might be trying to develop a collaborative culture.

In balkanized cultures, teachers are divided in different groups with whom they often socialize, creating tightly insulated associations that reinforce their views about teaching, discipline and learning. This type of association leads to poor communication and disputes among groups of teachers that does not grow into opportunities for learning and usually gets stuck in personal conflicts. Contrived collegiality can start as an *arranged collegiality*, a kick-start to begin developing collaborative practices among teachers when there is none, but if it does not evolve to more genuine collaborative practices, based on common values and understanding, it can become an administrative and bureaucratic prerogative endeavor. As Hargreaves and Fullan (2012) clearly argued:

> *collaborative cultures require some guidance and intervention. But this supports, facilitates, and creates opportunities for teachers to work together. Collaborative cultures don't mandate collegial support and partnership through fear mongering and force. (p.119)*

A professional learning community is characterized by the continuing work and relationship of educators that share a collective responsibility to improve their own practices, committed, respecting and caring for each other (Stoll, Bolam, McMahon, Wallace, & Thomas, 2006). The driver of the community is students learning and their own professional learning to better informing their own teaching practices. The idea is that everyone in the community should benefit from their joint process of reflection is not limited to quick solutions to complex educational problems. There is a persistent challenge among the participants to improve, and a sense that the learning is not only a goal but also a constant process (Hargreaves & Fullan, 2012).

In addition to these categories of within-school collaborative cultures, Hargreaves and Fullan (2012) also introduce a between-school category, designated with the broad label of Cluster, Networks and Federations. Networks have different types of collaborative process and practices and, arguably, by articulating professionals from different contexts, and even sometimes from sectors beyond education, collaboration can become more complex. Thus, promoting a collaborative culture, should both consider the complexity of collaboration not only within schools but also between and beyond schools (Chapman et al., 2016a).

COLLABORATION IN SCHOOL NETWORKS

There are two important conditions that underpin school-to-school collaboration: first, a commitment to share knowledge and willingness to actively participate in joint activity between different actors and, second, a clear shared purpose and sense of direction for the collaboration (Muijs, West, & Ainscow, 2010). Based on the work of Ainscow and West

(2006), Chapman (2015), Duffy and Gallagher (2016), Katz and Earl (2010) and Warren-Little (1990), we present four types of collaboration in networks with different characteristics: Association, Emerging Collaboration, Sustained Collaboration and Collegiality.

- *Association*: These are traditional work patterns with incidental meetings, usually initiated through a hierarchy that require schools to initiate a collaborative process. In these cases, there is no exchange of knowledge or resources. Collaboration can be observed as people relate ideas or experiences in response to an external mandate. There are occasional contacts among the participants where there is a general exchange of ideas, anecdotes and experiences, very similar to what Warren-Little (1990) identifies as *scanning and storytelling*. This can be an initial stage to then develop a more consolidated network. At this moment, it is important to create relationships among participant, to develop their professional trust, establish norms, negotiate and agree on shared values and define clearly the purpose of networking.

- *Emerging Collaboration*: This is an activity focused on short-term tasks. Those who collaborate do it to solve a problem, usually external or externally defined. In this scenario, it is easy to identify the challenge that congregates participants and to reach collective agreements because the task at hand is very specific to address. In essence, the external problem is the sustenance of the network. This is a form of collaboration where people support each other without challenging each other, avoiding interfering with each other's work.

- *Sustained Collaboration*: A more stable form of collaboration, supported by a set of common values and commitments to share knowledge, resources and practices. In these networks, long-term goals have been defined, and there are joint activities. Sharing successful and unsuccessful practices is key, and participants put their own work forward to be examined by others in pursuit of improvements. The capacities of its participants can be developed in the network, and there might exist an external support but that role is not a condition for the implementation of the network activities.

- *Collegiality*: Long-term commitment supported by a shared vision and set of common values. In this case, there is an evident distribution of leadership for the governance and activities of the network. There is an infrastructure and resources that allow the constant development of the network to achieve its goals. In these cases, participants share and understand a clear organization of work, so it is important that these networks also develop a monitoring process of strategic goals and how they are being achieved. Participants of the network regularly understand their own professional work as a collective responsibility involving professionals from communities other than their own and view the success of their work based on the learning of all the students who belong to the schools of the network.

These categories help to distinguish what it means to develop a collaborative network and what can be expected when a government purposefully promotes collaboration among different schools. However, it might seem from these categories that all networks should aspire to achieve collegiality, but that is not necessarily an appropriate goal for every network. Instead of understating these categories of collaboration as levels, they are different types of networking. PLN can be located in the sustained collaboration or collegiality categories, as they are expected to mobilize and produce knowledge among participants. Educational networks are dynamic and complex organizations, it is possible that they could progress to a stage where they achieve their goals, and it no longer makes sense to continue its operation, or they can decide to merge with other networks (Ehren & Perryman, 2018). Therefore, some networks might start as associations and work toward achieving emerging goals, without needing to develop a sustained collaboration or collegiality, and not all school networks will become PLNs.

Despite the benefits of collaboration, researchers have identified some negative aspects of collaboration (e.g., Peter-Koop et al., 2003). These challenges have been referred to as the "dark side of collaboration" and include:

1. *Illusion of association* – Passive buy-in creates the illusion of collaboration as a "sleeping partner."

2. *Fabricated cooperation* – Pursue one's own agenda to enhance power, status or resources, often at the expense of others.

3. *Collaboration with the "enemy"* – Initial engagement to control damage limitation and influence the agenda to mitigate perceived negative consequences of the collaborative activity. However, despite intentions this often turns into collusion. One becomes trapped by the dominant discourse and taken in by it.

4. *Contrived collegiality* – False public expression of values and belief systems that do not match the behaviors enacted by leaders or those involved in the collaboration. Particularly prevalent where unequal power relationships in bureaucratic hierarchies (Chapman, 2019, p. 7).

These rather negative dimensions of collaboration are an important reminder that not all collaboration is successful or that not everyone engages in collaborative activity with sound motives. These remain under-researched areas and for the most part, there continues to be an uncritical assumption that collaboration per se is a "good thing" that is likely to lead to positive outcomes. There is a need for further studies of failed attempts at collaboration and collaborations that have not delivered on expectations.

Looking back to the Chilean experience, Ministry guidelines for SIN suggest that network members should develop a sense of collective responsibility, fostering relationships of trust and developing a governance structure that will allow them to be more autonomous to decide the type of actions or projects they will engage with in order to achieve their network goals. Nevertheless, SIN guidelines do not suggest any kind of systematic or coherent methodology that networks could use to implement those collective actions or projects; rather, it was expected that the Ministry supervisor and network participants will be able to find the best practical methods to mobilize the knowledge of their network. Considering the dangers and ineffective practices that the *dark side of collaboration* can generate for collective endeavors, the absence of formal methodologies is clearly a weakness of the strategy, and it also makes particularly challenging to analyze how SIN promote (or not) a culture of collaboration.

The description of different types of collaboration helps to better understand that collaboration is very complex at school and network level but is far from granting a solution. It seems necessary to have a more specific methodological framework to mobilize knowledge and support collaborative practices among network participants. With that in mind, we propose *collaborative inquiry* as a suitable methodology for SIN, as it is based in similar values and principles and provides a more structured scheme that can help to analyze the development of collaborative processes in a PLN.

COLLABORATIVE INQUIRY

Collaborative inquiry, practitioner research and action research have a long and established tradition that can be traced back to the psychologist Kurt Lewin's (1946) work at MIT. In the United Kingdom, Laurence Stenhouse's (1975) work on curriculum development popularized this action-orientated work. The idea of the reflective practitioner (Schön, 1984) and the power of emancipation and the role of action research in educational change was promoted by John Elliot (1991) and others. These ideas were taken up by early school improvement researchers and activist and became the basis of the highly influential Improving the Quality of Education for All (IQEA) school improvement program developed at the University of Cambridge in the late 1980s and early 1990s (Hopkins, Ainscow, & West, 1994). This program influenced teachers, leaders, researchers and activists throughout the 1990s to the current day. This initiative was the genesis of the national "Networked Learning Communities" program in England (Jackson & Timperly, 2006). IQEA spread from England to Wales and could be found operating in diverse contexts across the globe ranging from Hong Kong to Iceland. The legacy of this program forms the basis of many contemporary research–practice partnerships using various forms of practitioner inquiry and collaborative action research within and across school networks.

This history and tradition has demonstrated that various forms of collaborative inquiry can be particularly valuable for school networks. For example, according to Ainscow

(2016) and Chapman et al. (2016a), a significant aspect of school-to-school partnership is that they can challenge deep beliefs of its participants, foster collaborative ethos and even reduce competition among schools of the same district. This methodology assumes that teachers' practices are part of the public domain, therefore can be publicly analyzed and improved. Also, for successful collaborative inquiry processes, it is crucial that leaders value the personal knowledge that professionals acquire in their everyday practice and to use these experiences to foster collective professional learning (Ainscow, Dyson, Goldrick, & West, 2016).

According to DeLuca et al. (2015), collaborative inquiry in practice is often confused by school leaders and teachers with assessment and evaluation of their practices. For example, two authors of this book have been researching a collaborative inquiry project with principals and curriculum coordinators participating in networks in Chile, and when they start inquiring into teaching practices, instead of researching collectively, including teachers in the process, they rapidly start to evaluate them. In these collaborative inquiry projects, principals and curriculum coordinators try to detect data to support preconceived ideas, instead of reflecting about data, with teachers, regarding what and how can teachers improve their practices (Pino-Yancovic et al., 2019).

Assessing and evaluating involves making judgments, which can be carried out with different purposes and methodologies (Greene, 2006; Segone, 2011; Tarsilla, 2010). Performance evaluation is usually a formal system that allows measuring compliance with functions, responsibilities and determining the effectiveness in achieving goals (Mizala & Romaguera, 2002). In the case of the evaluation of teachers' performance, it usually involves evaluating knowledge, behaviors and the outcomes of these in terms of students' learning (Tejedor, 2012). As previously highlighted, there is a long history of using various forms of collaborative inquiry to support the development of professional practices, to better understand and influence the teaching and learning process (Carpenter, 2017; Emihivich & Baglia, 2000; Hadfield & Chapman, 2009; Reason & Bradbury, 2001; Stoll et al., 2006). This form of professional learning and improvement activity does not seek to judge the practice of leaders and teachers. On the contrary, evaluative judgments interfere with the inquiry process, since they often paralyze reflection and learning. To carry out a successful collaborative inquiry, one must have an openness to learn with others, and avoid evaluating the work of those with whom this process is carried out.

PRINCIPLES AND VALUES OF COLLABORATIVE INQUIRY

Collaborative inquiry is a cyclical process in constant development and privileges the construction of knowledge located and conducted by the educational agents themselves (Reason & Bradbury, 2001). Intuition and judgments of school leaders and teachers are valued and very useful to promote collective reflection (Noffke, 1995). It is important that the questions that mobilize the inquiry are generated by participants in order to guarantee that it is their interests that prevail in this inquiry process (Anderson & Herr, 2007). Therefore, this methodology requires that those who assume roles to support this methodology value the knowledge of teachers, so the inquiry can help the development of their professional learning (Ainscow et al., 2016).

Collaborative inquiry assumes that the knowledge generated about educational practices is always partial, and even if it can be temporarily successful, it will be incomplete and subject to revision. In this sense, a key value of this methodology is to consider that the practice of teachers and leaders is a public issue that can be improved (Ainscow et al., 2016). This implies that there is no "recipe" to deal with the challenges that schools face, but rather teachers and leaders themselves are the best suited to find the answers to their own problems. There are a series of principles that should be considered in order to carry out a successful collaborative inquiry (Brown & Poortman, 2018; Chapman et al., 2016a; Stoll et al., 2006):

1. *Take risks*: Those who embark on this methodology are willing to take actions that do not have a guaranteed successful outcome. The idea is to learn from error and success. Dare to innovate with new strategies and evaluate the revision of practices by others.

2. *Generate, analyze and use a range of data to inform and understand the practice*: The use of data is valued as an important source of information for analysis and reflection. This means that data can be generated collectively and that there is interest in investing time to collect and analyze meaningful educational data.

3. *Build positive relationships*: Collaborative inquiry is carried out through a set of steps and strategies, but it is fundamentally a social process, which depends on the relationships that exist between the participants. Trust, respect for others and active listening are very important for this process to be successful. Therefore, collaborative inquiry requires a special dedication of time.

4. *Professional leadership opportunities for its participants*: The purpose of the inquiry must involve its participants. It should be especially visualized how this inquiry will be useful for the teaching–learning process and for the professional development of those involved.

Therefore, it is relevant that it be led by different people. Collaborative research involves developing a distributed leadership where joint work is carried out.

The SIN guidelines seem to recognize all these principles, but the guidelines are not explicit about clear and concrete strategies to support network members to preform practices inspired by those principles. For instance, the guidelines are not straightforward about how network members and supervisor can build a positive relationship base on trust to encourage participants to take risks together. Schools in Chile have access to a lot of diverse data that are produced by the Quality Assurance Agency, such as student outcomes, enrollment, attainment, family and student perception of the school. Nevertheless, often principal and curriculum coordinators do not have the capacity to analyze these data, and they lack skills to generate other kinds of local meaningful data to their own particular context. In part, this book aims to study SINs in order to better understand and analyze the collaborative practices that their members are able to engage in and what kind of knowledge is mobilized between and within school members of a network.

THE COLLABORATIVE INQUIRY CYCLE

There are different proposals to develop a cycle of collaborative inquiry. DeLuca et al. (2015), based on a meta-analysis of more than 60 publications on this methodology, conclude that there is agreement in the academic community that this is a cyclical process and that it is based on a socio-constructionist perspective about learning. That is those who study and propose to develop cycles of collaborative inquiry, consider that learning and knowledge are based on experience and constructed collectively. In addition, they identify three central features: (1) identification of common challenges, (2) inquiry and taking action; and (3) monitoring and reflection. The cycle can be seen in Fig. 4.

The movement between each one of these phases allows to generate a continuous process of innovation and improvement for professional practices. To facilitate the use of this cycle to analyze the SIN strategy, we describe each one of them in more detail.

Identification of Common Challenges

The first phase of the cycle involves generating a dialogue among participants, where values and beliefs about an area of improvement are made explicit. For instance, the dialogue to initiate the inquiry process can be linked to the curriculum, instructional practices and the process of learning of all students. It is essential that the focus of inquiry is shared

Fig. 4.   Collaborative Inquiry Cycle.

and relevant to all participants. Holmlund, Deuel, Slavit, and Kennedy (2010) argue that the willingness of teachers and leaders to engage in conversations is crucial to developing a collaborative inquiry cycle. Therefore, they must be "active subjects" of the inquiry and not be "objects" of the inquiry.

To identify common challenges, Holmlund et al. (2010) distinguish how conversations should begin as a dialogue and then evolve into a discussion. A dialogue occurs when people try to understand the meanings and ideas of others about a particular situation. This is an active process, where people are expected to ask questions to understand the perspective of others and avoid judgments. The discussion can be generated after the dialogue, where the participants are committed to an idea, take a position on a topic and thereby try to influence others to consider that their approach is relevant at the time of inquiry, which involves negotiating and challenging beliefs. The idea is that participants will commit themselves to a meaningful goal. The essence of this process is to centralize the diversity of interests in a very specific challenge. This initial work takes time and energy, but the evidence indicates that it allows for the inquiry endeavor to be valuable and useful for its participants (Ainscow, 2018).

Inquiry and Taking Action

The second phase of the cycle can take two different forms: an inquiry to generate data or an action to test strategies or methodologies that affect teachers' practices. These two distinct processes are part of the same phase because, as DeLuca et al. (2015) argue, generating data is already a form of action.

Also, taking action does not necessarily involve developing a new action because it can be an inquiry of a current project that already is being implemented in schools. For example, when leaders interview or survey their teachers about if they feel valued in their institution, they are not only collecting a form of data but also mobilizing the organization. The same applies when leaders are monitoring teachers' practices, which also influence teachers' behaviors and practices. Generating data is a strategic action for school leaders, which can activate the initiation of changes and improvements in their institutions. The value of collecting data is a subsequent analysis, otherwise all the time spent generating data can be wasted. Often, many instruments, including questionnaires or surveys, are administered in school, but it is challenging to find adequate time for analysis. Therefore, it is vital to plan the analysis of data at the start of the inquiry cycle (DeLuca et al., 2015).

Bernhardt (2013) distinguishes between data, information, knowledge and contextualized knowledge, each level involves a more complex data analysis. As Schildkamp, Poortman, and Handelzalts (2016), Zoro, Améstica, and Berkowitz (2017), and Zoro, Berkowitz, Uribe, and Osorio (2018) point out, the collection and analysis of data is a systematic, methodical and continuous process that needs to be completed by transforming the information into contextualized and actionable knowledge in order to support the decision-making process. It must be done intentionally to address some shared challenges.

For DeLuca et al. (2015), the new actions are carried out mainly by teachers on the teaching and learning processes. Innovating is not necessarily a revolutionary activity in the classroom, rather aims to test strategies that have not been carried out before and analyze the way they are carried out. Actions in this cycle require that teachers can experiment with new methodologies, that their educational practices are public and that their results are subject to scrutiny (Ainscow et al., 2016). School leaders need to generate the conditions for this to happen. Mistakes, doubts and errors must be valued and not penalized for the purpose of understanding and improving teaching and learning, in the logic of collaborating in a share inquiry, and not to evaluate teachers' practices.

Monitoring and Reflection

The third phase consists of monitoring and reflecting based on a shared analysis of the production of data or the action taken in terms of its execution or its effects and results. In this sense, DeLuca et al. (2015) highlighted that this should not be thought of as the final phase of a cycle of inquiry. In fact, under the logic of a (nonlinear) cycle of inquiry, a team of professionals can begin by analyzing the practices they have already applied in their schools, and then depending on the outcomes of such analysis, restart the cycle by identifying a new challenge that mobilizes new actions.

This analysis can be immediately enacted after the performance of one or several actions, as a moment to stop and reflect on the reasons that explain their results. Wohlstetter, Malloy, Chau, and Polhemus (2003) mention that this flexibility of collaborative inquiry facilitates the generation of shared knowledge among professionals from different schools. Collaborative inquiry is not limited to specific student learning outcomes or a specific time frame (e.g., a term or the school year). Its extension depends on the challenges posed by a group of professionals. It is relevant that when each cycle of inquiry is completed, future inquiries or actions are planned, so that collaborative inquiry remains as a continuous process of improvement and innovation. As the group advances in the inquiry, it is relevant for leaders to emphasize the milestones that the group achieves, in order to keep the motivation to advance toward solving or better understanding the educational challenges of the group. Evidence suggests that to generate substantial innovations in school networks, where professionals develop bonds of trust and a culture of collaboration, the continuous implementation of these cycles should have at least a duration of three years (Chapman et al., 2014, 2016a; Chapman & Muijs, 2013).

COLLABORATIVE INQUIRY AND PROFESSIONAL CAPITAL

A collaborative inquiry methodology for school networks seems to be appropriate to support the mobilization of knowledge and to develop collaborative practices among network partners. Our assumption is that a school network that properly adopts and implements collaborative inquiry cycles, or a similar methodology, needs to develop a level of sustained collaboration or collegiality. This can be a practical way of translating the concept of "culture of collaboration," which is the national declared goal of the SIN strategy. Each phase of the collaborative inquiry cycle helps to better identify the types of practices and knowledge that are present in SIN. For example, using collaborative inquiry as a framework, we could recognize if SINs can promote dialogue among their members in order to identify common challenges, or if they perform joint actions and inquiries about their practices, and finally, if SIN members engage in a collective analysis of their actions, for the generation of shared knowledge.

As described in Chapter 1, MINEDUC developed SINs in parallel to the strategy of Direct Visits to low-performing schools in order to ensure school leaders develop professional capacities to improve the quality of the educational system. However, this might not be enough to facilitate school leaders' capacities for collaboration as it stresses an individual approach to support.

In contrast to the MINEDUC's rationale, we assume that if SINs are able to implement complete and meaningful collaborative inquiry cycles, then the professional capital of network members can be developed. Professional capital is central for the systemic improvement of education, where all members of one network are collectively engaging to support the quality and equity of education, including local authorities and supervisors (Chapman et al., 2016a; Hargreaves & Fullan, 2012; Shirley, 2016).

Professional capital integrates three interrelated dimensions: human capital, social capital and decisional capital (Hargreaves & Fullan, 2012). Human capital started to being developed as an economic concept, related to the investment that can be done in people's education and the consequent financial return of that education for a corporation or business. In education, it has been mainly related to the knowledge and skills that teachers have to promote students' learning, if there is an investment in supporting the human capital of teachers, then, as a consequence, students will learn more and better thanks to those teachers. Now the concept has also evolved to teachers' feelings toward and knowledge of their students, and not only their training, and the concept also includes the "skills, knowledge, empathy, passion, confidence, charisma and leadership [of teachers and leaders]" (Chapman et al., 2016a, p. 180).

Social capital is directly related to the sharing of practices and knowledge among educational professionals (Díaz-Gibson, Civís-Zaragoza, & Guàrdia-Olmos, 2014). As Hargreaves and Fullan (2012) argue, "social capital increases your knowledge – It gives you access to other human capital. It expands your network of influence and opportunity" (p. 90). The central idea is that beyond formal training, teachers' social interactions impact in great ways their teaching practices (Campbell, Osmond-Johnson, Sohn, & Lieberman,

2017; Reid, 2014). Social capital has always been present for teachers, and as Hargreaves and Fullan (2012) argue

> *every time you increase the purposeful learning of teachers working together, you get both short-term results and long term benefits as teachers learn the value of their peers and come to appreciate the worth of constructive disagreement. (p. 91)*

Decisional capital is directly connected with principals' and teacher's agency. Decisional capital involves the possibilities that professional have to influence others and to apply their judgment into their everyday practices. When teachers can use this capital, teachers can choose the best educational practices to teach to their students and exercise this power in their schools and classrooms (Campbell, 2018; Chapman et al., 2016). In networks, this capital is crucial, because it is connected with how network members can decide and influence the definitions of the network purposes and actions.

Collaborative inquiry cycles that actively involve educational agents, within, between and beyond schools are privileged spaces to support the professional capital of its members. Consequently, our rationale is that SINs that are able to go through the collaborative inquiry phases are promoting the professional capital of its members and, with that, supporting the systemic improvement of education. In Fig. 5, there is a representation of this rationale.

Building upon these assumptions and rationale, the next chapter describes the mixed-methods study that was conducted based on the collaborative inquiry framework, for which we have conducted two independent studies: first, a primary multisite case study of 15 SINs in five regions of Chile and, second, a supplementary national study of principals and curriculum coordinators from 398 SINs active in the country. The analysis of the data helps to better understand the challenges and possibilities for the development of school networks in a market-oriented educational context that challenges the sustainability of these networks as collaborative spaces oriented toward systemic improvement.

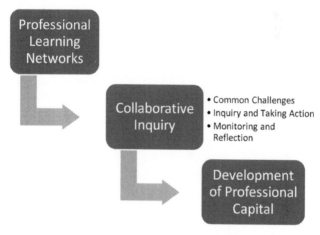

Fig. 5. Rationale of PLNs and Collaborative Inquiry to Develop Professional Capital.

3

A NATIONAL MIXED-METHODS STUDY OF SCHOOL NETWORKS IN CHILE

Mixed-methods research is a contemporary trend in the social sciences, and many controversies exist within this field regarding its nature as an integrative research paradigm (Creswell, 2011; Greene, 2007; Teddlie & Tashakkori, 2010). According to Creswell (2011), a strong controversial is the questionable use of qualitative and quantitative descriptors to define what mixed-methods is. It is understandable that this division between qualitative and quantitative paradigms exists within mixed methods. To a great extent, this is a result of the debates that took place during the 1970s and 1980s when researchers in both camps strove to make their respective methods the standard for studying social phenomena (Greene, 2007). However, while this dichotomy may make sense on an abstract or theoretical level, it does not seem as relevant in practice, as researchers tend to use both methodologies in the same study to understand a social phenomenon (Creswell, 2011).

Even when we look at a method in an isolated manner, as it is the case in content analysis, the qualitative versus quantitative distinction can become hazy. Some types of content analyses observe the repetition of certain terms, focusing attention on comparative frequencies and patterns of meanings. In this process, one must first perform interpretive hermeneutic work (qualitative) to codify words and meanings and then count these codified repetitions (quantitative). Finally, this analysis may take a qualitative direction, as in demonstrating the importance of a word or its meanings in a certain context. However, one could also create a histogram based on the frequency of each repeated word to find which terms are most prevalent, processes which can be understood as quantitative. Arguably, both analytical strategies are a combination of qualitative and quantitative (Creswell, 2011).

To resolve the tension mentioned above, some mixed-methods authors have spoken of a continuum between qualitative and quantitative (Creswell, 2008, 2011). Although this continuum addresses this tension, it seems that instead of solving the problem, it further reinforces the idea that mixed methods should use these two descriptors (qualitative and quantitative) to define itself.

Another issue with using the qualitative and quantitative methodologies to define mixed methods is that it creates an oversimplification that obscures the variety of ways to study social phenomena. In the case of qualitative methodologies, one can identify many different ways to conduct a qualitative study. For example, Schwandt (2000) presents three different epistemological perspectives – interpretivism, hermeneutics and social constructionism – within qualitative inquiry. Also, quantitative methodologies, that might seem more similar and appropriate for one unique paradigmatic tent, can also respond to different approaches to social phenomena. For example, descriptive statistics and social network analysis might all use quantitative data, but they are very different to be just reduced to the same quantitative category.

One way to avoid the terms "qualitative" and "quantitative" as primary descriptors in mixed methods is to focus on the purposes for mixing methods, rather than fixating the discussion on the methods mixed. In this area, Jennifer Greene has been recognized by her peers as a key researcher (Creswell, 2011; Johnson & Gray, 2010; Teddlie & Tashakkori, 2011), and her work has contributed significantly to rethinking mixed methods without limiting the field to an opposition (or a continuum) between qualitative and quantitative.

Greene (2007) describes mixed-methods research as a way of thinking with the overall purpose of better understanding a social phenomenon. Greene characterized this way of thinking about mixed methods as inviting "multiple ways of seeing and hearing, multiple ways of making sense of the social world, and multiple stand positions on what is important and to be valued and cherished" (p. 20). Among the variety of perspectives contained within mixed methods, one can pinpoint several paradigmatic positions that have an impact on methodological designs. This book is positioned in the substantive theory paradigmatic stance, the theoretical concepts that guide methodological decisions are most relevant for this stance. The phases of collaborative inquiry constitute the framework to mix the findings of two independent research studies about the SIN policy, where three of the authors participated. Following this logic, mixing depends more on the substantive theory, and the most logical thing to do is to strive for coherence between the guiding theory, research design and methods (Greene, 2007).

In this book, our purpose is to better understand the collaborative practices and knowledge that are mobilized in SINs, especially to identify if the SIN strategy is promoting a culture of collaboration in the competitive environment of the Chilean educational system. To achieve this goal, we employ the theoretical framework of collaborative inquiry to identify specific practices evidenced by these school networks.

MIXED-METHODS DESIGN

Following Greene's (2007) perspective, this mixed-methods study's main purpose is to better understand to what extent SINs have created the conditions for the development and sustainability of meaningful collaborative practices among network participants, and the production and sharing of relevant knowledge within networks. Three research questions have been defined to structure the design of this mixed-methods research: (1) What kind of knowledge is mobilized between the SINs and the schools that compose them? (2) What types of meaningful collaborative practices among school leaders can be promoted by the SINs in the Chilean market-oriented educational system? (3) What are the challenges and possibilities for the development of sustainable school networks in a market-oriented educational context? Each of these questions addresses different topics that are key for Professional Learning Network (PLN), the first focused on *knowledge mobilization*, the second on *collaborative practices* and the third on the *sustainability of networks*.

Despite the three research questions have a clear focus, they are still too broad. To access precise, concrete and relevant information from both studies, these three general questions have been broken into more specific key questions. Using the collaborative inquiry cycle as a substance theory to mix our methods (studies), the key questions are located into each phase of the inquiry cycle. The design of the mixed-methods research is described in Fig. 6, where the general topic, the key questions and the phase of the collaborative inquiry are presented.

This mixed-methods study is composed by two independent studies, primary and supplementary (Greene, 2007). The primary study is a multi-site case study, consisting of interviews, focus groups and observations with participants of 15 networks to understand how the SIN policy was designed and implemented

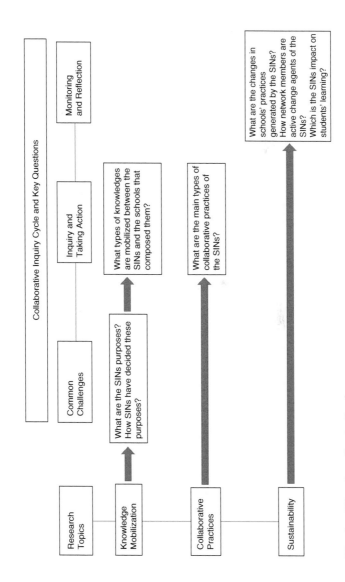

Fig. 6. Mixed-methods Design.

in 2016. Findings from this study are presented in chapter 4 as the primary source of data for the mixed-methods analysis of the SIN strategy. The supplementary study is questionnaire applied nationally in 2017 to collect information about the functioning of SINs from the perspective of principals and curriculum coordinators. A summary table of findings from the questionnaire is briefly introduced in this chapter to present an overview of the three-factor structure of the instrument, which is employed to characterize network functioning. Later, in Chapter 4, we use specific data from questionnaire items to support and complement the data presented by the primary study. Next sections describe the rationale, design, participants and instruments of the multi-site case study and the national questionnaire.

A MULTI-SITE CASE STUDY OF SIN

In 2016, MINEDUC sponsored a multi-site case study to analyze the key elements of the design and examine the early implementation of the SIN strategy in the country, with financial and technical support from the Santiago office of the United Nations Educational, Scientific and Cultural Organization (UNESCO). The study was conducted by a team of researchers led by the Pontifícia Universidad Católica de Valparaíso, in collaboration with researchers from the Center for Advanced Research in Education of the Universidad de Chile and from the Universidad de Magallanes.

The research team designed and conducted a multi-site qualitative case study (Stake, 2005) of 15 networks in five regions of the country (Coquimbo, Valparaíso, Metropolitana, Biobío and Magallanes) focused in different Provincial Departments of Education. These departments are centrally coordinated by the General Education Division of MINEDUC and consist of a variable number of supervisors, who are the ministry's representatives in each network of the territory. The number of supervisors working in a given Provincial Department of Education depends on the population in the territory where these are located.

The specific objectives of the multi-site case study were (1) identify the purposes, action plan and rationale of the SINs; (2) identify and characterize conditions and areas of enactment of the educational practice of the SINs; (3) contrast MINEDUC's design of SIN strategy with its implementation in the chosen territories; and (4) describe strengths, opportunities for improvement and learnings that arise from the implementation of the SINs, identifying (a) SINs' contribution to the enactment of collaborative practices between leadership teams that participate in the SINs and (b) SINs' contribution to improving school management practices.

The fieldwork was conducted between July and November 2016. The study involved two stages of data collection and analysis. The first included an individual interview with staff from the Provincial Department of Education, specifically the chief of each department and technical-pedagogical chiefs from the networks; an individual interview with local administrators (municipality or private-subsidized administrator) and an individual interview with ministry supervisors who participate in each of the networks of this study; and the analysis of official technical documents of the MINEDUC related to the SIN strategy.

The second stage included an individual interview with a principal and a curriculum coordinator who actively participated in their SIN, and a focus group was conducted with principals and curriculum coordinators who participated in the studied SINs. These individual interviews and focus groups were held with 10 out of the 15 studied networks, lasting 70 minutes on average. Finally, two observations of the work sessions of each of the 15 SINs were performed, lasting approximately 90 minutes each.

Diversity in terms of the number of participant schools, their administration (municipal or private-subsidized schools), their location (rural or urban) and type of schools (elementary, academic high schools, vocational high schools) were the main criteria to select the cases. The majority of the selected networks (11) consisted of schools administered by a municipal department of education. Nine networks convened schools belonging to one municipality, one network consisted of schools from two municipalities, two involved five different municipalities, two networks were composed of schools from six municipalities and the largest network involved schools of seven different municipalities. The smallest network was composed of 6 schools, and the largest of 16, on average, school networks were composed of 10 educational institutions. All networks included elementary and high schools, seven of them included also vocational education and one network was only composed of special education schools, which are educational institutions that only serve students with special education needs. In Table 1, there is a full description of the characteristic of each studied network:

The observations and protocols for individual interviews and focus groups were based on a theoretical framework consisting of several areas and dimensions relevant for networking (Ahumada, González, & Pino-Yancovic, 2016): (1) orientation to improvement (purpose, processes and sustainability), (2) organization of the network (actors, nodes, type of relationships, distributed leadership, structure and support), (3) social capital (reciprocity, centrality, trust and collective responsibility) and (4) network trajectory and socio-historical and cultural context. Data were analyzed for each network case, and then a cross-case analysis using qualitative content analysis was performed (Cáceres, 2003) with the software Atlas ti. The cross-case analysis was guided by a list of codes based on the theoretical framework and emergent codes that seemed especially significant from the information provided by participants.

Table 1. Characteristic of the Studied SINs.

Network Number	Municipality	Administration	Urbanization	Grades of the Schools	Number of Institutions
SIN 1	5	Municipal and privately subsidized	Urban and rural	• Kindergarten • Elementary • High school • Vocational training	11
SIN 2	5	Municipal	Urban	• Kindergarten • Elementary • High school • Vocational training	15
SIN 3	1	Municipal	Urban and rural	• Kindergarten • Elementary • High school • Vocational training	2 (4 rural)
SIN 4	1	Municipal	Rural	• Kindergarten • Elementary • High school	6

(Continued)

Table 1. (*Continued*)

Network Number	Municipality	Administration	Urbanization	Grades of the Schools	Number of Institutions
SIN 5	1	Municipal	Urban	• Kindergarten • Elementary • High school • Vocational training • Special education	7
SIN 6	1	Municipal	Urban	• Elementary • High school • Vocational training • Adult education	9
SIN 7	6	Privately subsidized	Urban	• Kindergarten • Elementary • High school • Special education (language)	15
SIN 8	2	Privately subsidized	Urban	• Kindergarten • Elementary • High school • Special education (language)	11

SIN 9	1	Municipal	Urban	• Kindergarten • Elementary • High school • Vocational training • Special education • Adult education	8
SIN 10	1	Privately subsidized	Urban	• Kindergarten • Elementary • High school • Vocational training	13
SIN 11	1	Municipal	Urban	• Elementary • High school	9
SIN 12	1	Municipal	Rural and urban	• Elementary • High school	6
SIN 13	1	Municipal	Urban	• Elementary • High school	16
SIN 14	1	Municipal	Urban	• Elementary • High school	13
SIN 15	7	Municipal	Urban	• Special education	10

During this multi-site case study, the research team developed two reports of the findings that were turned to the study counterpart at MINEDUC. This study provides rich descriptions of the operation of SIN that could be deepened when looked at with other evidence about these networks. Nevertheless, being an exploratory case study limits the possibilities for generalization from its findings.

SIN NATIONAL QUESTIONNAIRE

The second study has been developed since 2016 by our team at the Leadership Center for Educational Improvement, LIDERES EDUCATIVOS, at the Pontificia Universidad Católica de Valparaíso. Each year since, we have been monitoring nationwide the perception of principals and curriculum coordinators about their SINs, employing an adaptation of the Educational Collaborative Network Questionnaire developed by Díaz-Gibson, Civís-Zaragoza, and Guàrdia-Olmos (2014).

The adapted version of the questionnaire measures network functioning based on three theoretical dimensions: professional capital, networked improvement and networking. Professional capital considered the three interrelated areas described previously in this book (human capital, social capital and decisional capital). Networked improvement is assessed based on how participants perceive the effects of the networks in the improvement of their schools, with special emphasis on individual and collective outcomes of networks (Leithwood, 2018). Networking is focused on the perceived functioning of the network, with emphasis on the purposes, agenda and projects being carried out within networks. These dimensions are assessed with 32 Likert-type scale items asking school leaders about their level of agreement with a given statement about their SIN. The questionnaire also has five open-ended questions inviting principals and curriculum coordinators to express their views on (1) aspects that facilitate networking, (2) aspects that hinder networking, (3) support received from their network, (4) contributions to their network and (5) advice to improve networking.

For the mixed-methods research reported in this book, we have considered data from 2017, collected between July and October through an online platform. An email with a cover letter and a link to the questionnaire was sent to principals and curriculum coordinators of the 483 networks actively operating that year in the country. During the application process, these participants were contacted by telephone to confirm they received the email with the link to the questionnaire and encourage them to answer it. Finally, a total of 1,789 school leaders, who participated in 398 networks, answered the questionnaire.

DESCRIPTIVE ANALYSIS OF THE NATIONAL QUESTIONNAIRE

In the 2017 application, the majority of participants identified as female (63%), half of them were principals (54%), and a significant proportion identified as curriculum coordinators (40%). Only a small group indicated occupying another role in their schools (6%). Due to the adaptation made of the original instrument (Díaz-Gibson et al., 2014), an exploratory factor analysis was conducted to test the validity of the dimensions theoretically measured: networking, professional capital and networked improvement. The Kaiser–Meyer–Olkin (KMO) test confirms the adequacy of the survey data for such analysis (KMO = 0.986).

Assuming, as the theory suggest, that the three factors (dimensions) are correlated, Table 2 shows the loadings by factors and items using promax rotation. The correlation matrix of the promax-rotated common factors confirms correlations between factors of 0.671 and 0.688. Using a minimum loading

Table 2. Rotated Factor Loadings, by Items and Dimensions.

	Networking	Professional Capital	Network for Improvement
In my network we evaluate how our work contributes to our schools' improvement	0.66		
In my network, there are norms for dealing with conflict that arise as a result of differences in opinions	0.65		
My network contributes to solve problems at our own schools	0.60		
In my network, we have created new knowledge by searching for solutions to shared issues	0.60		
My network established mechanisms and communications channels to link up with community actors and institutions	0.59		
In my network, we have shared responsibilities among its members	0.58		
In my network, there are leaders who help resolve differences in opinion and internal conflicts	0.56		
My network facilitates the development of skills and professional development of its members	0.55		
My network's agenda is developed based on the priorities and interests expressed by its participants	0.54		
The members of my network share their schools' practice to achieve our network objectives	0.52		

Being in the network fosters a shared view for defining our network needs	0.50		
My interest to participate in network meetings has increased since the first meeting	0.48		
The members of my network participate actively in the planned activities	0.45		
In my network, I feel I participate at the same level as other members		0.73	
In my network, the opinions of principals and curriculum coordinators are equally respected than those of general members		0.72	
In my network, I feel there is trust to freely express my perceptions and disagreements		0.68	
The decisions made in my network are agreed among its members		0.60	
The tasks in my network are carried out by teams including professionals from across all participating schools		0.50	
In my network, there are spaces of trust and mutual understanding among members		0.47	
I participate in the decision-making process of my network		0.47	
My network favors cooperation among its members		0.47	
School networks contribute to share resources among participant schools		0.37	
Participating in the network has improved my leadership skills			0.75
My network helps me find solutions to problems that I face in my school			0.70

(Continued)

Table 2. (Continued)

	Networking	Professional Capital	Network for Improvement
The members of my network understand that the work done is fundamental to improve school management			0.64
I feel very committed to the work we do in my school improvement network			0.61
The actions of my network are organized to address students' educational needs			0.61
The ideas that arise from my network have been implemented as actions or projects in my school			0.56
The participation of the members of my network contributes to the work done in my school			0.53
I use the knowledge generated in my network in my school			0.53
My network promotes that all members are creators of new ideas or projects			0.52
The topics discussed in my network are appropriate to the school context where I work			0.41

threshold of 0.40, results indicate an adequate simple structure of the questionnaire measuring the three dimensions. Additionally, the uniqueness indicators for each item range from 0.15 to 0.42, thus showing that all items in the questionnaire would be sufficiently explained by these common factors.

The three dimensions show high and similar internal consistency in the Cronbach's alphas (networking: 0.97, professional capital: 0.94, and networked improvement: 0.96). Networking is the lowest rated scale (mean = 4.80), networked improvement shows a better rate (mean = 4.88) and the highest rated scale is professional capital (mean = 5.10). The percentages of agreement and disagreement by item in each dimension are described in the Appendix.

One of the limitations of this study is the self-selection of respondents and the effect this could have in their responses, school leaders who did not answer the questionnaire can be different from those who did answer it. This potential response bias was anticipated by explicitly asking the participants for their perceptions of both positive and negative aspects of the SIN strategy, and by reassuring that all responses would be treated anonymously. However, self-selected surveys do not ensure a proper generalization of the result, and they need to be taken with some caution when there are no other data sources about the same phenomena that could be employed to contrast and compare.

MIXING PROCEDURE

While the multi-site case study provides in-depth data from different stakeholders involved in the design and implementation of SIN, it only focused on 15 cases. In the other study, the questionnaire strength is its large scope, collecting data about the perception of SIN considering 398 out of 483 networks, with 1,789 individual responses. However, it is only focused on principals and curriculum coordinators, and the main data are structured in a Likert scale. Considering the weaknesses and strengths of both studies, they complement very well, and their mixing helps to generate a good portrait of the SIN strategy during the years 2016 and 2017.

The design of each study was aimed at meeting their own objectives, and it was not anticipated to mix their data. Therefore, in order to produce a coherent analysis of the SIN strategy based on evidence from these two studies, we devised an ad hoc substantive theory mixed-methods research, guided by collaborative inquiry as a theoretical framework (Greene, 2007).

Following this paradigmatic stance, the collaborative inquiry phases were used to mix the findings of each study and answer our general research questions, which were broken into more specific key questions, in a two-stage process. First, findings from the primary study (multi-site case study) were analyzed to respond the key questions, using thick descriptions and concrete examples of the SINs. Second, findings from the secondary study (national questionnaire) were revised to determine the spread of the primary study findings in the country and also allowed to add supplementary information to answer the key questions. Fig. 7 represents the procedure of the mixed-methods research presented in this book.

The three phases of collaborative inquiry were used as deductive categories to analyze the data and inferences of the multi-site case study and the SIN national questionnaire. Also, considering the literature review of collaborative inquiry, themes for each category were defined, and emergent themes were created based on the revision of the studies. Next, Chapter 4 describes the findings of this mixed-methods research.

Fig. 7.   Mixed-methods Procedure.

4

SCHOOL NETWORKS: FROM COMPETITION TO COLLABORATION

In this chapter, we describe and analyze the experience of implementing the School Improvement Network strategy in Chile. We employ the findings from both studies, the primary multi-site case study and supplementary national questionnaire, and mix the data and inferences emerging from each independent study. We do so using key questions, organized in each of the three stages of the collaborative inquiry as organizing theoretical framework. Thus, we present the evidence of the implementation of SIN in regard to (1) the identification of common challenges, (2) inquiring and taking action and (3) monitoring and reflection.

For each phase of the collaborative inquiry cycle, themes were created based on specialized literature and topics emerging from the findings of each study. In addition, in the final section of this chapter, we present a short reflection about the challenges that SIN should address to better support a collaborative culture that can foster the development of professional capital for its members.

IDENTIFICATION OF COMMON CHALLENGES

This phase of the collaborative inquiry cycle involves generating a dialogue and debate among participants, which then should evolve into a definition of the network purpose and goals. Two key questions related with the topic of *Knowledge Mobilization* are addressed in this section: (1) What are SINs' purposes? and (2) How SINs have decided these purposes?

At this stage of the collaborative inquiry, participants are expected to engage in a conversation about their values and beliefs regarding a particular area of improvement in which they are interested in making an impact. This conversation is expected to lead to a dialogue trying to understand the meanings and ideas of others about this particular phenomenon. A common challenge supposes a shared understanding about an educational issue that participants define as useful to change, by taking actions or to inquire collectively.

Our findings indicate that there is a variety of purposes identified for each network: (1) dissemination and analysis of national policies relevant for schools, (2) development or implementation of national key policy instruments (e.g., review of school climate policies, especially to confront bullying in each school, an analysis of the new citizenship education national program and an analysis of what can be understood as an inclusive education and how to address students with special education needs) and (3) the development of professional capacities by sharing educational experiences. Additionally, participants from some networks of the multi-site case study declared that they have not yet defined a clear purpose for their network, apart from the dissemination of official information about ministry policies.

The purpose defined by these networks reflects the knowledge identified to be mobilized among network members. Some networks from the multi-site case study are not very specific about the knowledges to be mobilized, but they do state that they have analyzed diverse pedagogical topics relevant to schools' PME. This finding is coherent with the supplementary study, the national questionnaire, where a great majority of respondents declared that a main concern of networks is analyzing the management of the pedagogical aspects of each schools' PME.

Finally, there are three ways in which network members defined their purposes: (1) a definition of common goals based on individual and collective performance conducted by principals and curriculum coordinators, (2) supervisor with school leaders conduct an analysis of schools' performance and use that data to decide which are the main weakness and strengths of the network and then decided a common goal for the entire group and (3) the purposes were defined by supervisors considering their experiences and their own analysis of the schools that participate in the network.

Analyzing the SIN strategy regarding this phase of the collaborative inquiry cycle, two important themes emerge. First, there is evidence that one key issue for these networks was *establishing a common purpose,* especially in the early days of the strategy. In this theme, we discuss in detail the content of the definition of purposes and knowledges identified and valued by network members. Second, evidence from the two studies also suggests that *negotiating SIN purpose among partners* became a key milestone for the formation stage of these networks; in this item, there is a description of three processes in which networks decided their purposes and knowledges.

Establishing Common Purposes

Evidence from the multi-site case study indicates that the main purpose of most of the studied networks relates to the *dissemination and analysis of national education policy* to schools to address challenges that they identify as collective. In this sense, the definition of network purpose is nuanced or complemented according to the particular characteristics of each partner and how each supervisor adapts the national strategy to their local context. For instance, in a network of secondary schools, while a wide set of policies are transmitted to principals and curriculum coordinators, they emphasize those associated with the development and strengthening of leadership professional capacities, so that they can effectively mobilize competences in their teachers in order to have an impact in their classroom practice. In this case, the purpose is associated with the development of principals' and curriculum coordinators' skills and knowledge for instructional leadership, selecting and deepening in certain specific policies related to this topic.

In other networks, the purpose is related to the *implementation of national key policy instruments*. For instance, in two networks of rural and urban primary schools, the purpose of the network is focused on taking advantage and share the existing knowledge of each school to solve pedagogical issues they face in their contexts. These pedagogical issues are, in turn, closely related to specific policy guidelines promoted by the Ministry of Education regarding the design and implementation of each school Educational Improvement Plan (PME). Furthermore, for some cases, the purpose of the network is nothing more than informing and disseminating ministry policies to school leaders in the context of specific reform aims, such as policies concerning *school climate and bullying*, *citizenship education*, *inclusion and special education needs* or policies related with *the reform of public education in Chile*.

Conversely, in a few cases, the purpose has no obvious link with specific ministry policy; however, they were framed by the larger process of reform that was taking place in Chile, where the SIN strategy was conceived. In these cases, the purpose had to do with the *development of professional capacities by sharing educational experiences and projects between schools*, building trusting relationships to facilitate, in the long run, the development of collaborative projects between the partner schools. For instance, in two large networks of urban primary and secondary schools, they engaged in a process of sharing their individual experiences, successful and unsuccessful, as a way of opening up to partners and overcome the competitive relationships they had established until then.

In general, staff from the Provincial Department of Education, specifically the chief and technical-pedagogical chief of each provincial department, have a similar understanding about the SIN purposes. This purpose ranges from disseminating new educational policies to developing professional learning communities by creating conditions for school leaders to share and analyze educational experiences and projects. The representatives of local administrators (municipal or private subsidized) also have a similar perspective about SIN purposes, but they have conflicted judgments about these purposes. For example, a director from one municipal department of education explains how SIN general goal is to share successful educational experiences that will improve student learning:

> *I believe that the objective was to take advantage of successful experiences of some schools, and to make them public, so others can take advantage of them, or use them in a very productive way, to change what they do, the other schools that do not have those practices (...). It has been positive, because in some way [school networks] make possible to know*

> *other ways of working, and experiences that are*
> *implemented, educational projects and initiatives*
> *from different schools, and that, in the end, is*
> *favorable to improve students' learning. (Director*
> *of Municipal Department of Education, SIN 3)*

There are other representatives of the local administration who disagree with the purposes of SINs about disseminating educational policies or that were critical about the possibilities of SINs to promote the sharing of experiences among network members. This is mainly because of the great amount of network meeting time dedicated to discussing educational policies. For these network members, there are *no clear purposes besides of being part of informative meetings* guided by ministry educational supervisors.

Principals and curriculum coordinators have different understandings about SIN purposes and also about the value of those purposes. This variety of perspectives is evident between the different cases studied. For some, networks have a clear and shared meaningful goal. Others state that they are not aware of the specific objectives of their network but have a general understanding of their purpose and value very much the opportunity of networking. And a small group is in direct disagreement with their network's purposes and operation. The following quotations represent each of the three perspectives about networks' purposes:

> *The network allowed us to realize that we are in*
> *the same place, that is, we have the same problems*
> *of school climate, the same problems of leadership,*
> *we have the same problems in the curricular*
> *management, therefore ... we are the same, and*
> *we can work together to address these problems.*
> *(Principal, SIN 4)*

> *[The purpose] has never been explicit, as in a
> program, but it has always been implicit, that the
> network should give special relevance to vocational
> high school education. (Principal, SIN 1)*

> *I believe that the network's management model is
> poorly designed, it seems to me that the purpose is
> not responding to what we need, which is mainly
> closer support to our own educational needs and
> goals. (School Improvement Plan Manager, SIN 7)*

Data from the national questionnaire provide evidence
that principals and curriculum coordinators consider the
purpose of their networks to be appropriate and consistent
with the challenges they face in their schools. For instance,
40% agree and 43% strongly agree that the issues addressed
in their network are relevant to the educational context in
which they are inserted.

This perception suggests that network participants are committed to working on a specific area of educational improvement that is consistent with the challenges faced in their
schools as a collective. However, data from the survey also flag
some areas of concern regarding the perception of the practical
value of the purposes defined in SINs. For instance, 15% somewhat agree, while 8% somewhat disagree, disagree or strongly
disagree that the action of their networks contributes to developing a shared vision about their collective needs.

Considering the data of the multi-site case study and the
national questionnaire, it is possible to argue that, in general, participants value the opportunity of networking, and
it seems that they make use of the network space to address
the challenges they are facing. However, in this initial stage of
implementation, the SIN strategy guidelines failed to explicitly address the importance of coupling the dissemination of

policies with the purposes for each network, beyond the sharing of educational experiences by each school. The neglect of this critical issue generated disagreement in some participants to what they perceived as the instrumentalization of networks by the central government to disseminate information about educational policies. Moreover, this was not always in a way that was meaningful or valuable for its members, misusing the time of principals and curriculum coordinators to support the development of their professional capacities. In this regard, the literature highlights that centralized networks that do not promote collaboration and participation incite resistance instead of professional learning (Greany & Ehren, 2016).

Negotiating SIN Purpose among Partners

There is evidence from both studies that illustrate how SINs come to define their purpose, as part of a process of network formation where expectations and aspirations of different stakeholders come together. The diversity of purposes shows the complexity of each network and how purposes were proposed, negotiated and defined.

Networks that clearly define their main goal as the development of professional capacities by sharing experiences are also much more democratic to define their purposes. At least two process can be identified, one where participants agree and *define common goals based on individual and collective performance* and another based on a *sophisticated consultative process* led by supervisors, using the priorities of schools' members and an evaluation of the network. The following quotes illustrate both processes:

> *In the network we looked at some schools'*
> *performance and how they were trying to*

*improve, and those that were actually improving
substantially in the SIMCE [national standardized
test] (...) then there was a time to reflect how
and how much those school were improving
(or not improving). Then, what we saw is that
schools that were improving, they systematically
implemented a reading plan, then this topic
[reading plan] was analyzed in the network, and
participants agreed that it was actually a very
good plan, and the collective decision was that
as district it would be valuable to work together
in the reading plan and currently a teacher from
each school is participating in a professional
development training program about the reading
plan. (Principal, SIN 4)*

*In the general planning, an analysis of the previous
year is performed, an instrument is applied for us
to evaluate our achievements as a network, and
at the same time we discuss what are our interests
and needs, then a document that consolidates both
the evaluation and schools' interests is written,
participants choose priorities. Finally, based on
all this work, the MINEDUC supervisor decides
the monthly program and activities for the year.
(Curriculum coordinator, SIN 1)*

Some principals and curriculum coordinators describe
that, initially, purposes established by the MINEDUC were
adjusted in relation to the characteristics and changes in
the local context and to the network's own trajectory. In
relation to this, thinking about and reaching an agreement
about a common purpose for the network has been, in
most cases, the first big challenge and meaningful change

about the network dynamics that they had to face as a collective:

> *One objective was that the meeting was not only prepared by the ministry supervisor, which was initially as it started. But after a while, participants, from their own point of view, started to share experiences that they considered successful, and that could serve others, so people can know about their institutions, but also, so those experiences could serve as a model for others, and so a meeting plan for the year was generated. I feel this plan has been very productive for the group. (Principal, SIN 10)*

Something similar happens in SIN 2, where rather than sharing practices, school leaders are interested in strengthening their leadership skills but argue that this purpose is not shared by all partners in the network, and that the *purpose of the network was defined by the supervisor*. Here, school leaders suggest that a big obstacle for advancing their purpose in the network is the unidirectional and vertical approach of the ministry supervisor, leading to a lack of spaces for conversation about strategic guidelines that can carry their expected purpose of the network.

Data from the national questionnaire confirms that participants have been able to define shared objectives related with their own school practices. In that regard, 36% strongly agree, 43% agree and 14% somewhat agree with this item reflecting that schools share their practices to achieve network objectives. Also, about the decisions that are made in the network, a majority of the participants agree that they are part of the decision-making process, specifically a 31% strongly agree, 40% agree and 17% somewhat agree, and there is only a 5% of disagreement (aggregating all levels of disagreement).

Participants who responded to the survey seem to have a positive perception with regard to the relation between network objectives and topics of relevance for their school. They also consider themselves part of the decision-making process of their network, which might imply that they have, to some extent, an influence on these goals. Nevertheless, 16% of principals and curriculum coordinators only somewhat agree, while 18% somewhat disagree, disagree or strongly disagree that the agenda of their network is defined according to the priorities and interests manifested by them. These results might be indicating that the majority of respondents feel that they can influence the decision-making process of the network, but a relevant group of participants do not perceive themselves as having ownership over network goals, despite that networking activities are related to the individual goals of their educational institutions.

Data from both studies suggest that networks started as a one-way road and are instrumental for disseminating national educational policies. This instrumentalization of the networking space by powerful actors with vested interests has been reported elsewhere in the literature, where mandated networks could impinge schools' autonomy to advance governments' agenda (Mifsud, 2016). However, evidence about SIN shows that after some time of operation only few networks have continued that path. In fact, the studied cases and responses to the survey indicate that a great majority of the networks have turned into spaces where participants could share and discuss professional experiences, increasing their active participation in their network. As both studies represent the state of the SIN strategy after two years of implementation, this seems as a fairly positive change, but it is evident that networks require a strong and clear methodology to consolidate this change toward deeper collaboration in networks, in order to effectively enact a cultural change.

INQUIRY AND TAKING ACTION

The second phase of the collaborative inquiry cycle consist of the collective action that network partners can perform to produce data or to test new practices. An essential element of networking is the development of actions leading to collaboration and knowledge mobilization among schools and with other networks. If networks cannot perform concrete practices, all the time and effort invested in the first phase would have been misused. Thus, it is crucial that networks define precise actions that promote positive and relevant changes among partners, with a dedicated focus on transforming practices at the school level.

Two main questions related with the topic of *Knowledge Mobilization* are addressed in this section: What types of knowledges are mobilized between the SINs and the schools that composed them? Also, one question related with the topic of *Collaborative Practice* can be identified at this stage: What are the main types of collaborative practices of the SINs? When analyzing the SIN strategy using data from the two studies, we see that this phase has been approached very differently within networks, depending mostly on the value that network partners have given to networking.

Evidence from both studies shows a range of knowledges that are mobilized among partner schools within networks, but there is less evidence in both studies about the knowledges that are mobilized between SINs and schools. Regarding the type of knowledge that is mobilized among network partners, some refer to formal contents that school leaders should analyze. Also, participants mention that they develop knowledges and skills to enhance the quality of schools' PME. Finally, in some networks, participants collectively analyze reading plans and share pedagogical themes defined by schools' PME objectives. Concerning the knowledges that are mobilized between SINs and schools, the scarce available evidence suggests that participants identify and replicate actions initially witnessed in their networks and bring them back into their schools (e.g., increase the effectiveness of collaborative practices among teachers and activities with the local community).

In the multi-site case study, school members declare that the main collaborative practice was sharing successful or innovative experiences and educational projects. Some networks developed collective or common projects based on data, preforming joint actions. An interesting collaborative practice was a regular informal collaboration, observed in many networks, where members shared tips during coffee time.

In the following subsections, we present three themes emerging from the analysis of data. First, a detailed description of how some networks perform the main action of *dissemination and inquiry of educational policies* and the value that network partners assign to this informative activity. Second, we introduce evidence about how some networks managed to move forward and develop *collaborative practices among school leaders* that was mostly based on the sharing and exchange of practices and resources between principals and curriculum coordinators. And third, evidence is presented about how networks have engaged in the *mobilization of knowledges*, where partners collectively think about and implement actions leading to expand and disseminate the knowledge and resources of the network to their schools or, in some cases, to other networks.

Disseminating and Inquiring of Educational Policies

As we described in the previous section, networks focus their action on disseminating national education policy to its

partners, complying with the rules of operation of the network strategy and paying special attention to the regulatory
aspects of education. Far from this being a problem, many
participants appreciate that the information about policies
was very valuable to better understand national guidelines
for school leaders and how different schools from the same
territory are responding to them. This was a good starting
point for network partners to open up about their practices.
Also, some principals value the involvement of ministry
supervisors in their networks when they present and discuss
current educational reform topics because that allows principals to engage in conversation with an official representative
of the government, facilitating a fluid communication and
a better understanding of the meaning and implications of
national policies. In general, participants value the quality of
the information received, usually accompanied with material
resources such as guides or practical management tools that
facilitate their everyday work and that, in many cases, were
able to apply in their schools:

> *The information comes directly from the source,*
> *that is, official ministry information is delivered*
> *by the source, I mean, they give it to us right here*
> *[in the network] that makes us come to network*
> *meetings, always willing, because bottom-line*
> *you are going to get information, an update, and*
> *then they give us materials, they send a lot of*
> *information via email too, so that helps quite a*
> *lot, to improve both management and pedagogical*
> *practices in our schools. (Principal, SIN 5)*

Data from the multi-site case study networks provide evidence that advice and information are fundamental not only
to review and improve pedagogical practices among partner

schools but also for the development of skills and knowledge of principals and curriculum coordinators. In this context, the role of both the local administrator representative and the ministry supervisor is central for these informative processes. Networks that have focused their action on learning about policy and management instruments emphasize the training and development of technical skills associated with the implementation of such policy. Two policy documents that many network members describe as valuable and that they analyzed collectively were the *Good Principalship and Leadership Framework* and the *Citizenship Education Plan*. The first is a document that provides guidelines about the expected good practices of principals in Chile, while the second was part of a recent reform enacted when this research was being conducted:

> *We started, eh, first reflecting on, about our occupation, but secondly, we had, eh, something like a self-training, peer-training, because we will not always have an expert coming in, we do have each other. And we did this analysis in a previous meeting about the changes to the Principalship Framework, for instance, a new area was included, a new element, and it is not enough to know that now there are four or five, but to analyze it and when we did we saw that a principal's field of action is both wide and very specific. (Curriculum coordinator, SIN 2)*

Principals highlight that the exchange of experiences and projects about *pedagogical issue related to their PME* was especially valuable and relevant for network partners because they were able to revise each other's plans and introduce innovations based on the work of others:

*One does a lot of exchange, "what are you doing
about this? What activities have you considered?",
etc. And that is where one gets ideas for innovating
too, because since the PME has goals at four years,
but each year you review it in some way some
aspects, then one does not want to enter in the
routine of every year doing the same thing, so we
support each other in that "How are you doing it?
Ah, we are doing this." And those little things
we take back to schools. (Curriculum coordinator,
SIN 10)*

Nevertheless, organizing SIN activity around providing
information about educational policies is not without its
problems. In some cases, participants describe that they are
unable to use this knowledge because of the bulk of direc-
tives, practices and guidelines, which overwhelm participants
with excessive information, making very difficult to prioritize
the most relevant knowledge that can result in changes in
their schools. Evidence from the cases shows that networks
where informative processes predominate feature unidirectional relationships oriented to the transmission of technical
knowledge. In these networks, there is a clear tension between
the role traditionally fulfilled by ministry supervisors visiting
schools individually to review and assess their progress and
their role as facilitators of collaboration among participants
in the network:

*Schools are topped with stuff and I don't know
why they get so full with things and in the end the
important stuff is not prioritized, so, these things
are left aside, because there is also something of
a distant relationship between the Ministry and
schools. Then, at the end these pieces of paper we*

> *are given we file them [...] we are given information*
> *and that information is staying. (Curriculum*
> *coordinator, SIN 5)*

The use of networking time to address management
issues is also reported by the national survey, where 90% of
respondents agree (34% strongly agree, 39% agree and 17%
somewhat agree) that the work done in their network is fundamental to improve school management. In the open-ended
question of the national questionnaire about the support that
participant received from the network, a common response
is *technical knowledge to improve the quality of the PMEs*,
which allowed network participants to enhance their pedagogical leadership knowledge. Technical knowledge is relevant for principals and curriculum coordinators because they
connect this knowledge with improving teachers' practices
and student outcomes. At the same time, in the open-ended
question about what they would suggest to improve their networks, a majority responded that they desire to strengthen
the collaborative work among partners, which indicates not
only that principals and curriculum coordinators value collaboration but also that maybe some network foci have been
narrowed to analysis of policies and policy implementation.

Collaborative Practices among School Leaders

This second theme describes the types of collaborative practices
that were observed in the multi-site case study and backed
up by network participants' responses to the national questionnaire. Some networks simply started their collaboration
by sharing experiences, but then this evolved to establish common interests and, eventually, coordinated action. Principals
and curriculum coordinators also value the opportunity of an

informal collaboration, one that is not part of the official network meeting, but it is very relevant for their everyday work.

In the multi-site case study, we found several types of collaborative practices. For instance, one type emphasized the sharing of successful or innovative practices, where the focus is on educational improvement processes, understanding this as an opportunity for network partners to think about how to change and innovate in their own practices:

> *Practices began to be shared, that is networked collaboration, why? Because those schools that managed to achieve their goals, and this is also thanks to the impulse from supervisors, we started to see, well, if this school is making it, why not help and share these experiences with other schools, so we saw that and invited schools that had positive results. (Provincial Department of Education technical-pedagogical Chief, SIN 2)*

An essential element for the implementation of this collaborative practice is the development of trusting relationships between partners in the network. In these cases, evidence shows that ministry supervisors have been relevant to create an environment that fosters and provides incentives for partners to share their practices and what they have learned from their experience. In this type of networks, there is a concern with knowing what is being done in each school in order to connect partners with similar interests or with complementary needs and expertise:

> *[We proposed] to show a successful practice about school management, or about classroom work. They accepted that proposal, and we started this form of participation in the network where each school presents their successful experience. But it*

took some time for them [ministry supervisors]
to understand that partners also needed a more
active participation, not mere receivers of what they
wanted to introduce. That is now consolidated,
implemented, and will continue in the next
semester. (Representative Municipal Department of
Education, SIN 9)

This year we implemented a sign-up system
where you pick a topic linked to what you were
developing in your school, I remember picking
the arts education topic because it is what we
are working on in my school and it is what I like
to present, and each one was picking what they
wanted to present about their schools, which
is a real exchange of practices. (Principal,
SIN 10)

This evidence suggests that, in these networks, collaboration consists of taking advantage of the expertise available to develop cooperation among partners. The development of these collaborative practices in networks followed a general process. First, there is an analysis of data of each school; second, an assessment of how each school has progressed in achieving their goals, in terms of not only student outcomes but also about teachers' practices related with management and leadership; and third, a collective analysis of the network goals, with the aim that participants share experiences and ideas that support the development of those collective goals:

We started with an analysis of how we are doing,
and we looked at qualitative and quantitative
information, we analyzed it and reached a
conclusion of how we are doing. We look at SIMCE
scores, internal learning assessments, and so on.

> *Then, I moved on to [discuss] what do we want as*
> *schools because I wanted to introduce the relevance*
> *of the educational institutional project. (Ministry*
> *supervisor, SIN 3)*

Few networks have successfully agreed on shared objectives. These networks operate with a shared work plan, and their collaboration implies knowing each partner's expertise and develops actions toward a common objective. Evidence also shows that few networks have been able to organize their action for collaboration, and when they do it has been either for obtaining and enhancing their resources or for the implementation of very specific joint activities.

For instance, partners in a small network of urban and rural primary schools have designed and implemented a *reading plan* based on the *collective self-evaluation of their students' attainment* in this area and the selection of the most effective teaching strategies each partner contributed. Another network of municipal and private-subsidized vocational high schools has organized its action around common issues regarding the development of vocational programs, enhancing its pedagogical work and its articulation with future employers through joint actions. In both networks, the role of the ministry supervisor has been to facilitate the conditions for partners to come together and contribute to the objectives in which the network focuses:

> *In our network we have a rotation for hosting*
> *meetings, we have had evaluation together, they*
> *[school leaders] exchange experiences, collaborate*
> *on issues even related to resources sometimes, they*
> *even pool some of it, offer their school building.*
> *For graduation they are supportive, and everyone*
> *is alert when they have a graduation or anniversary*
> *so they can be present as network and be with them*
> *for their event. (Ministry supervisor, SIN 1)*

Aside from these instances of collaboration, based on formal exchange and sharing of practices, the case study also offered evidence of *informal instances of collaboration during the development of network meetings*. For instance, during network meeting observations, our team picked up two specific moments of informal collaboration. The first took place during the coffee break and the second was at the end of the meeting. In both instances, participants talked in a relaxed and open manner about their concerns and shared advice and solutions to their problems. This is illustrated in an exchange during one group interview when network participants were asked about the sharing of mistakes and failure within their network:

> *P2: What you say is very important because I also learned from [name], from her experiences, then sometimes, in these things that are, perhaps, emerging in each of the schools, because one thing happens to you with parents or with the students, and suddenly another colleague can enlighten you and you think "if I do this, what happened to the colleague can happen to me." Those things I think are emerging. Sometimes more things come out during breakfast and you start talking to other people [...]*

> *Q1: What happens is that breakfast has become the space for reflection.*

> *Q4: It is more informal, and one feels more in confidence. Sometimes you relate to those who have more affinity, and you tell them your things.*

> *(Group interview, SIN 10)*

This positive attitude toward sharing advice and practices is also found in the results to the national SIN questionnaire.

For instance, 43% agree and 36% strongly agree with the statement that members of their network put at disposition of others their practices and those of their schools to achieve the objectives of the network, while 37% agree and 49% strongly agree that all opinions are equally respected in their networks. These results reinforce a sense of horizontal membership and freedom of expression, as well as the exchanging of experiences and resources between participant schools, which suggests that participants consider that they are sharing significant and meaningful elements for developing collaborative action.

Knowledge Mobilization between Networks and Schools

The third theme relates to how some networks have managed to mobilize some of the practices and expertise exchanged internally toward external agents and institutions. For instance, there is evidence from the multi-site case study where some networks have been able to mobilize knowledge about the *model of collaborative work developed among partners*, toward schools:

> *For example, the first entrepreneurship workshop was led by the high school, because its principal participated in an internship and learned about entrepreneurship in Europe where it is very popular, just like dual graduation. Then, the model shown by the high school was adapted by other schools, not only here in the district but elsewhere too. There was a transference there. They learned from us and we go on and strengthen ourselves based on others' experiences. There we can say there is a way to mutually benefit. (Curriculum coordinator, SIN 1)*

One critical element found in the case studies is the importance of active participation and commitment for enhancing the value of transferring network knowledge for school leaders and their organizations. In networks where knowledge is effectively mobilized toward schools or other spaces, people feel their participation was key. This belief is sustained in the assumption that there is always something positive to learn from others and if people actively participate in their networks, they will be able to recognize these positive elements and take them back to their own organizations:

> *I think that depends only on … how you take things, I think that the participation of each one of us, eh … the importance that you give to what you are doing, because I believe that in, in all the meetings one should take out good things and bad things as in every order of things, therefore it matters a lot the participation, that is to take the good and … and basically discard what, what is not useful, to be very clear about the situation. (Principal, SIN 7)*

Similarly, evidence from the case studies suggests that people hold commitment in high esteem within networks. Commitment is essentially viewed as the measure of effort and dedication that each participant displayed as partners in the network. This is mostly referred to when evaluating the way people assume the responsibility of taking on suggestions by other members of the network, or when partners host the organization of a network meeting, striving to make a good impression and making a serious effort to show the best they could offer to network partners. This committed environment has been supported by the action of ministry supervisors and is often seen by network members as a stark contrast with their previous experiences of sharing with their peers. The key difference is the positive attitude and willingness to open up to others' opinions with the goal of addressing mistakes and identifying learning and improvement opportunities:

> *I have spent a lot of time as a principal, so going or not going to a meeting, I do not win or lose, then when I go if the thing is wrong, I go quickly back to work at my school. But I feel that they [ministry supervisors] have managed to generate a commitment with the participants, and it shows a preparation, one sees that there is work, then you do not leave when you see that they work like this. I have raised issues on a couple of occasions and the next meeting we have discussed them, and if it has not been possible, they have also said it. (Principal, SIN 10)*

> *I believe that what we do is listen to the reality of each one and from there, rescue the positive, to integrate it into my school [...] I believe that sometimes, people work so closely and as they do not want to give much to know, what he does inside the school; one, because he does not want to be criticized, nor questioned, because to assume that one can be wrong, it is not easy and there are people who have a hard time assuming, who make mistakes or who are not doing, perhaps, what is best and the other thing is that there are usually people who simply do not like to share their experiences. (Curriculum coordinator, SIN 5)*

There are some examples of knowledge that has been mobilized into the schools. For instance, in a network of rural and urban schools, some school leaders explain that the *methodology and strategies employed during network meet-ings have been taken back by school leaders to work with their own teachers.* This has led school leaders to think about the importance of carefully organizing these work instances to facilitate the work with teachers. One principal describes his experience as it follows:

> *And the other thing that networks have, right? and at least what I've done already, what I've done, to me networking has also allowed me to improve the work I do to, uh, in the teachers' councils, ok? I [...] It has allowed me to mature, eh, the organization of these teachers' council meetings and they are not so much disorganized ... or, how to say it? so disconnected, I prepare them very well, very neatly, I have clear idea of what I want to achieve that day with my teachers? (Principal, SIN 4)*

Another example from the same network are activities that have been raised within network meetings but have evolved beyond the action of the network itself and turned into *projects involving other agents of the community.* As a result, these activities have gone beyond the traditional boundaries of education and linking to interests from the wider community where these schools are a part of. The representative of the municipal education department declared:

> *Not only remains here, but the community in general can perceive and know the work that has been done [within the network] The short film contest we developed, we call it "cinema under the stars" because we did it on a Friday night. So that this comes out and extrapolate what has to do properly with the schools, has helped make our work acknowledged [by the community],*

> *constantly, and people are motivated, besides,*
> *the fruit of their work [within the network] is*
> *reflected in a tangible result [outside the network].*
> *(Representative Municipal Department of*
> *Education, SIN 4)*

Despite the positive experience of this and a couple of other networks, in most cases, it has been very difficult to develop a strategy for transferring the knowledge and resources of the network to schools or other organizations. This is mainly because there is no strategy or methodology to facilitate this transfer, and it is expected that principals will just go ahead and do it on their own. Moreover, we found no evidence of specific training for ministry supervisors or representatives of municipal or private-subsidized administrators to produce such facilitation.

One way to address this issue is bringing outside professionals, such as teachers and others directly involved in educational improvement efforts, to network meetings as a way of facilitating the mobilization of network knowledge to other professionals and organizations. This is a very complex issue, as people need to consider not only who are the key people to invite to network meetings but also if the internal social conditions of networks would favor the occasional participation of external professionals. Nevertheless, some school leaders see this as a necessity to make the action of the network visible to outside people and organizations:

> *I think we need to do more, because we are the*
> *ones who pass down the information, and perhaps*
> *the network should invite the Mathematics teacher,*
> *the school counselor, or we could invite pre-school*
> *education, I do not know, I think there is an issue,*
> *we would have to increase perhaps the number of*

> *people and maybe say "well, today we are going*
> *to invite this person" so that they see what we*
> *are doing, because maybe they will think that we*
> *sit down to talk, we do talk, but we talk about*
> *education, We are not wasting our time, we are*
> *working and everything that is done here [network]*
> *is passed down there [schools]. (Principal, SIN 9)*

Finally, the national SIN questionnaire shows moderately high levels of agreement regarding the fact that people are effectively mobilizing knowledge produced in their networks toward their schools and other agents of the system. For instance, 44% agree and 21% strongly agree that the ideas that emerge from their networks have been implemented as actions or projects in their schools. This is an important level of agreement but not as high as with other items in the questionnaire, reflecting that there might be issues for SINs to actually mobilize knowledges between networks and schools. Similarly, 44% of respondents agree and 25% strongly agree that their network has generated new knowledge from the search for solutions to collective problems.

MONITORING AND REFLECTION

The third phase of the collaborative inquiry cycle consists of collectively review and think about the actions or inquiry taken by the network, in terms of its execution or effects, in order to produce an evaluation of its outcomes. As noted in previous chapters, this phase should not be considered as the end of the inquiry but rather as a point to think back, take stock and project how will the network move forward. In a nonlinear cycle of inquiry, the team of professionals can begin by monitoring the development of their action, so to reflect and evaluate their activities based on the outcomes achieved and restart the cycle by identifying pending or new challenges to mobilize new actions.

Three main questions related with the topic of sustainability are addressed in this section: What are the changes in schools' practices generated by the SINs? How network members are active change agents of the SINs? Which is the SINs impact on students' learning? As described earlier, the Ministry of Education intends that the SIN strategy would facilitate the articulation between the central, intermediate and school levels in order to build capacity for improvement based on a culture of collaboration. This implies that SINs should concentrate their action on enhancing the work that educators do in schools and particularly how school leaders who participate in these networks create appropriate conditions for this. As a result, monitoring and reflection in SINs should be driven by a shared analysis of the actions developed among network members and their effects in relation to teaching and learning in schools.

The mixed-methods analysis of the SIN strategy based on the two studies shows that this is the less-developed area of networks in Chile. However, network members demand more opportunities to provide feedback about the impact of network activities in the schools. The multi-site case study shows that principals and curriculum coordinators would like more power in the decision-making processes, which seems to be insinuating that they are not yet active change agent of their networks. Finally, being this the first and second year of implementation, there is no clear evidence of direct impact of SINs on student outcomes, despite evidence in the previous phases of how this strategy seems to be supporting the professional capital of participants in many SINs.

To present the results, first we describe how participants declare the importance of *developing formal strategies for collective reflection,* which they perceive as a critical to develop the necessary conditions for school leaders' engagement in networking as active agents and, as a result, strengthen their professional capacity as school leaders. Second, and similarly to what happened in some cases regarding the definition of networks' purpose, there is a need of being more precise in *identifying and evaluating network outcomes* in order to ascertain their effectiveness in terms of facilitating conditions for improved teaching and learning and inform adjustments to the SIN strategy that would allow to sustain networking over time.

Developing Formal Strategies for Collective Reflection

Despite that network members declare the development of collaborative practices within networks, and that observation of SINs corroborate such kind of practices, evidence from the multi-site case study suggests that networks often fail to develop formal instances for collective reflection and monitoring. Network participants are aware of the need to develop these instances to generate information about the progress of their actions and the achievement of their purpose. For most people, however, the latter seems to be less pressing than the former, as they perceive that network purpose is closely associated with the dissemination of educational policies in an informative way. Nevertheless, and as described in Chapter 1, national guidelines provided by the Ministry of Education for the SIN strategy state that networks should build from informative spaces where education policies are disseminated, toward more autonomous networks that would operate as Professional Learning Communities addressing common challenges for network participants:

> *Before we received the supervisors from the provincial department (...) and they made a presentation of a given topic (...) it was like bringing the information from the Ministry to schools, so they delivered and we took it up. Now this thing started to take form, it is like the beginning of a learning community sort of speak, because they (ministry supervisors) already know us and they can give us suggestions, together with the (municipal education) corporation, and say "look, in your school this strategy was successful, why don't you share it?", and we have developed enough trust for this to happen in our network. (Principal, SIN 5)*

Taking from the perspective and experience of the principal in the previous quote, the transition from an informative to a more collegial network arrangement seems to be supported by interpersonal trust and precise knowledge about what each school needs and can offer to the rest of the network. To develop these two elements, it is important that partners within networks (school leaders, local administrator and ministry supervisor) engage in collective reflection in order to deeply learn about and from others:

> *I think the most important thing is to install the reflection, express its importance. I think we are doing well, that is, we have shared a lot of reflective instances between the schools and us (ministry supervisors), I think that is fine. Understand that institutional management, school leadership are not ... fortuitous, it is not like someone touches*

> *with a magic wand and the thing starts working,*
> *but to understand that these are processes of*
> *knowledge and learning, of work, that require this*
> *system (networking) that if it provides a certain, eh,*
> *condition to, to take it seriously, eh, you can make*
> *it work. (Ministry supervisor, SIN 10)*

Nevertheless, evidence shows that this progression toward learning communities is restricted by certain conditions preventing network participants to engage in reflection about their collective action. For instance, regarding the leadership within networks, in general, it is centered around the figure of the ministry supervisor. As a consequence, participation within networks for other agents is restricted. In addition, the emphasis given by supervisors to the dissemination of policies offers little space for addressing schools' needs and interests:

> *I believe that the fact that it comes armed from the*
> *external system, that is the central level, I think it*
> *is difficult, because the actors could have a greater*
> *role if one felt that it is within the guidelines (for*
> *networking). We have never questioned that either,*
> *if you ask, perhaps it is also our responsibility,*
> *because we have never questioned as a network*
> *what our levels of autonomy are, how far we can*
> *go, what is sought. (Representative Municipal*
> *Department of Education, SIN 9)*

As a result of these discussions, it seems that the relevant issue within the context of this third phase of the collaborative inquiry cycle is having formal strategies for collective reflection within networks in relation to school change and improvement. *Participants demand more opportunities to provide feedback about the impact of network activities in the schools.* For instance, some school leaders express their desire to have some kind of feedback about their contributions to the network when sharing good practices as a strategy for their networks to better contribute to their work in schools:

> *I do not remember receiving any feedback, only the gratitude because it was very well evaluated [their presentation in the network], but at the same time there was not, that is, more than the good reception, but a feedback that said "look, here is what you can do" no, no. (Principal, SIN 9)*

Regarding the national SIN questionnaire, there is a slightly more positive view about the issue of developing the capacity for collective reflection within networks. For instance, 66% agree or strongly agree with the statement that their networks develop actions and strategies to evaluate how their work contributes to the improvement of participant school. However, 26% is undecided (somewhat agree and somewhat disagree) about this statement, and about 8% disagree or strongly disagree. These results suggest that a significant proportion of networks are not developing strategies to reflect and monitor about their actions as a collective and how these contribute to enhance teaching and learning in their schools.

Identifying and Evaluating Network Outcomes

A second topic associated with this phase of collaborative inquiry relates to the identification and evaluation of network outcomes, which are formally defined by the SIN strategy as the development of leadership skills and strengthening of schools' PME, through the facilitation of collaborative work and sharing successful experiences. This is a crucial issue for the SIN strategy, which ministry guidelines understand as network *depth* or *scope*; that is, in what ways networks produce effects on teaching practices and student learning in participant schools. However, in all the networks studied, it is stated that it is still too early to evaluate this type of results and even that there are *no clear indicators or objectives to evaluate the effect that the improvement networks are having*.

For instance, and as we described before, some networks offer no evidence of strategies to ensure the transference of information, knowledge and/or resources to their schools and teachers. The monitoring of network activities does not offer information about this, and it is only through direct visit to schools by ministry supervisors that they can make sure some of the issues discussed in the network are having some kind of effect in schools and, more specifically, in the change of classroom practice:

> *On the one hand, the issue of promoting teamwork in schools and ultimately improving the institutional practices of schools, why? because we know that management teams are rotating, then the challenge is how to make it [practices shared and agreed in their network] institutionalized, that is, part of the actions of the daily life of the schools and that in the end, if the supervisors are not there, they can do it alone […] What we lack is the evidence that all we discussed [in the network] happens in the classroom itself, because maybe all this can be worked on in meetings of reflection perfectly, and they are working on it, the different topics. But I do not know, we do not know, because we have not done it, if all this is really, how it is coming to the classroom. And the way of making sure if it is coming to the classroom, would have to be by checking their outcomes. (Ministry supervisor, SIN 13)*

Apparently, the most notable effects of networking have been at the level of leadership practices, facilitating increased collaborative work and sharing successful experiences in each network. This is a view that is mostly held by the ministry supervisors:

> *So the main objective of the network, is precisely to improve the skills of the management teams, through the development of leadership skills, and for that purpose we engage in the information and dissemination of policies, but also applying these in a contextualized way in schools (...) the objective is that in the end the school is autonomous, that it produces its own practices (...) generating a professional community of learning through autonomy within the school, and on the other hand also that as a district they can generate their own professional learning community. (Ministry supervisor, SIN 13)*

Data from the national questionnaire show a slightly more positive perception about the evaluation of the SIN strategy in its declared aim of strengthening school-level practices through a collaborative approach. For instance, 44% agree and 24% strongly agree that the participation of peers in network activities is contributing to the work done in their own schools; that is, a majority of school leaders perceive that instances of work with peers in their networks are a positive influence in their work.

Similarly, there is a positive perception about the other declared aim of the SIN strategy related with the development and strengthening of school leaders' competencies and skills. The development of professional capital, facilitating more collaborative work and sharing successful experiences in each network, seems to be the clearest outcome of the SIN strategy. For instance, 39% agree and 23% strongly agree that partici- pating in their network has improved their leadership skills.

Also, professional capital is the factor with highest rated scale (mean = 5.10), and as it has been previously described in the phase of inquiry and taking action, almost all the work of SINs has focused in the development of professional capacities of principals and curriculum coordinators.

SYNTHESIS OF FINDINGS

In general, the mixed-methods analysis suggests that SINs are, for the most part, responding to significant challenges that school leaders are facing in terms of implementing change and improvement strategies (PME). These professionals value the knowledge that is mobilized within their networks and, in some cases, they have transferred some of this knowledge and put it to use in their own schools. At this stage of implementation, however, there are only few experiences of collective projects being undertaken in networks as part of the SIN strategy, which is the ideal from the perspective of the collaborative inquiry framework, as most networks are dedicated to disseminate information and share experiences and practices.

Evidence presented in this chapter indicates that in the first two years of implementation, the SIN strategy shows positive signs. SINs have provided a space for school leaders to obtain information about and analyze meaningful policy instruments, such as guidelines to enhance school climate conditions or to reduce bullying and violence in educational settings. Evidence also suggests that SINs have defined common goals based on individual and collective performance, and some have applied consultative process, led by ministry supervisors, to define these purposes. The multi-site case study reveals that SINs have supported the development of professional capacities of principals and curriculum coordinators by sharing experiences and successful practices among partner schools. The national questionnaire corroborates these data, suggesting that this has been the main outcome of SIN in its initial nationwide implementation stage.

Conversely, the SIN strategy has proven to be less effective in mobilizing knowledge between networks and partner schools, although some knowledge has been transferred. These knowledges are very specific, centered on leadership contents, such as The Good Principalship and Leadership Framework (MBD-LE) and technical knowledge to enhance the quality of schools' PME. Also, networks have turned into positive environments to support the development of pedagogical interventions defined by schools' PME, such as the implementation of a municipality-wide reading plan. What seems to be clear is that at this stage, the main outcome of the SIN strategy has been the development of the professional capital of network members. This has been done by facilitating conditions for collaborative work based on members exchanging (successful) experiences in network meetings, either on formal or on informal instances.

There is less evidence, however, about how school leaders have been able to identify and replicate actions performed in their networks back into their schools. Nevertheless, data from the national questionnaire confirm that the ideas and knowledges that arise from networks are implemented as actions or projects in the schools. In the multi-site case study, there are some examples that suggest that participants have been able to use the methodologies and strategies employed during network meetings and take them back to their schools and use them to work with their own teachers.

Some concerning findings of this multi-site case study are that in some SINs most of the time is dedicated to disseminating information. This informative activity might be relevant, but it does not take full advantage of what a PLN can actually achieve. This happens particularly when the purposes of the network are defined by supervisors, without an appropriate negotiation or engagement with the needs of network members. This finding might be related with the requirement of some network members to have more opportunities to provide feedback about the impact of networks activities in schools and to have more power in the decision-making processes. Nevertheless, as these data represent the second year of implementation of the SIN strategy, in general participants are optimistic, and they profoundly value the opportunity of working with others.

To summarize, Fig. 8 presents the main findings of this mixed-methods study considering the key themes and each of the collaborative inquiry phases.

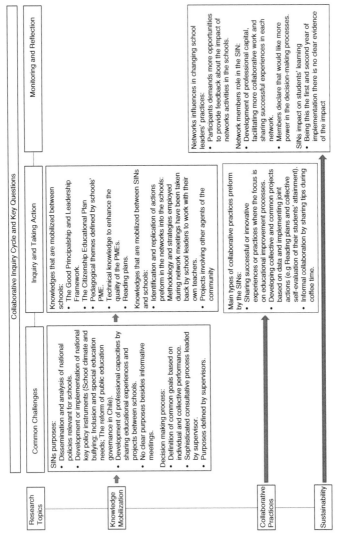

Fig. 8.   Mixed-methods Findings Summary.

5

SUSTAINABILITY OF THE SCHOOL IMPROVEMENT NETWORKS

Educational policies that seek to promote meaningful and positive changes need to include measures to become sustainable over time. One of the most recurrent recommendations for policymakers is to have a clear sense of direction, with a proper rational and rigorous evidence that supports reforms and national educational programs (Hargreaves & Fullan, 2012). Instead of going fast by escalating successful programs, the ideal is to understand the variations of policies in diverse contexts, actively involving the perspective of principals, curriculum coordinators and teachers (Bryk, Gomez, Grunow, & LeMahieu, 2015).

This chapter provides a reflection about the sustainability of School Improvement Networks (SINs) as professional learning networks, set in a particularly challenging context: the market-oriented Chilean educational system. For that purpose, first we discuss the development of conditions for effective Professional Learning Network (PLN) that has facilitated the development of *professional capital* among school leaders as a result of the SIN strategy. Then, we introduce the idea of network leadership, focused on practices that network members should apply to allow networks to be sustainable. In this section, we especially emphasize the relevance of leadership capacities for *leading downwards*, *lateral leadership* and *leading upwards*, mobilizing influence and power relations within and outside networks, which is crucial to sustain change in a challenging context. Finally, we argue that SINs, as professional learning networks, require a suitable *system infrastructure* to become a meaningful policy, able to change cultural patterns beyond the remit of networks themselves.

EFFECTIVE NETWORKS AND PROFESSIONAL CAPITAL

The literature identifies a series of internal conditions associated with effective networks. In this book, we highlight three of them: *purpose*, *collaboration* and *inquiry* (Brown & Flood, 2019; Chapman et al., 2016a; Duffy & Gallagher, 2016; Katz & Earl, 2010; Leithwood, 2018; Leithwood & Azah, 2016; Muijs, West, & Ainscow, 2010; Poortman & Brown, 2018; Rincón-Gallardo & Fullan, 2016). PLNs that define clear and ambitious collective purposes perform collaborative practices that facilitate knowledge mobilization between networks and schools by inquiring into their actions and results. Under these conditions, PLNs can prompt change processes in schools by inviting the development of positive changes in school leaders' practices and supporting their empowerment regarding strategies to improve education in their contexts.

The mixed-methods research presented in this book offers evidence that SINs have been able to develop some of the conditions required for the development of effective PLN. In general, SINs have defined a network purpose and performed collaborative practices consistent with such purpose. The process of defining this network *purpose* is based on individual and collective performance self-evaluation, and some have applied sophisticated consultative processes led by ministry supervisors to define their purpose. SINs have been able to analyze the development and implementation of meaningful policy instruments to support inclusion in education and enhance schools' climate to reduce bullying and violence in educational settings.

There is evidence from the multi-site case study and national questionnaire about how SINs facilitated participants to share experiences and practices, relevant for members to address educational challenges in their own schools. Nevertheless, a troubling finding is that some networks of the multi-site case study did not identify their network purpose. A clear, shared and specific purpose is crucial for effective networks and to develop valuable collaborative inquiry endeavors (Chapman et al., 2016a; Leithwood, 2018, Leithwood & Azah, 2016; Muijs et al., 2010; Poortman & Brown, 2018; Rincón-Gallardo & Fullan, 2016). Clear goals and outcomes are relevant for schools that participate in networks in competitive contexts (Armstrong & Ainscow, 2018). SINs as PLNs should specify the particular benefits, as well as the individual and collective learning goals that members can achieve in their networks (Brown & Poortman, 2018).

The findings of the mixed-methods research presented in this book reflect that SINs have been able to support *collaborative practices*, and that ideas discussed by network members in SINs have been implemented as actions or projects in their schools. In regard to the content, principals and curriculum coordinators work mainly on their Educational Improvement Plan (PME). This is a relevant national management document, and the use of this plan formalizes network activities, a practice that in other contexts has been indicated as relevant to support an institutional engagement of schools with their networks (Brown & Flood, 2019). In the multi-site case study and national questionnaire, participants highlight the value of the networks to analyze, improve and share pedagogical actions from their PME.

Though some networks show weaknesses in the definition of a shared purpose, SINs have managed to create a space for developing the *professional capital* of principals and curriculum coordinators. Findings from the multi-site case study and the national questionnaire show that SINs contribute to the development of social and human capital. Participants describe and declare an improvement in their leadership skills, that collaborating with other school leaders has a positive influence in their work, developing and strengthening of school leaders' competencies and skills. Despite some controversies, the process in which some networks have been able to decide about their purposes and themes, and how they have been able to decide about how to implement these ideas into their own schools, also reflects a development of their decisional capital. Professional capital is the factor with highest rated scale (mean = 5.10), and SINs have dedicated most of their activities, energy and time to support the professional capacities of principals and curriculum coordinators.

Notwithstanding the development of professional capital among school leaders participating of SINs, there is limited evidence about how they have applied this capital in their daily practice at schools, for instance, providing examples of changes produced as a result of transferring and employing network knowledge in their schools. In general, according to the national questionnaire data, the large majority of principals and curriculum coordinators claim to use network knowledge in their schools; however, the quality and nature of this activity remains obscure, as the mixed-methods analysis found no consistent evidence of this. In addition, the multi-site case study indicates that participants demand more opportunities to provide and receive feedback about the impact of network activities in their schools. This would suggest that the SIN strategy needs a more thoughtful and explicit methodology to support an *inquiry* processes about the projects that are shared in networks. Moreover, these networks need to progress from a stage of sharing practices to researching collectively. As Brown and Flood (2019) have previously claimed, and our mixed-methods analysis of the SIN strategy corroborates, the element of knowledge mobilization is the one that school leaders need more support to *get it right*.

SUSTAINABILITY AND NETWORK LEADERSHIP

Apart from the internal conditions associated with effective networks, PLN sustainability can also be analyzed in terms of the effects they have on partners within and outside their networks in support of the improvement of the quality and equity of education. In that regard, Hubers and Poortman (2018) indicate that PLN sustainability can be analyzed based on three criteria: (1) changes in the behavior and practices of school leaders related to their engagement in PLN, (2) changes implemented by network actors translated into positive outcomes for their institutions and (3) network members becoming active change agents, that is to say, empowered of the activities and destiny of their network.

To discuss these criteria in light of the mixed-methods analysis of the SIN strategy, we propose three network leadership capacities that can be associated with PLN sustainability: *leading downwards*, *lateral leadership* and *leading upwards*. We present these three capacities as part of a more complex practice of systemic leadership, which we understand as

> *An innovative practice of school leaders who*
> *seek to facilitate learning in school networks,*
> *as well as intensify the linkage and coherence*
> *between different levels of the School System.*
> *Systemic leadership is a key capacity to sustain and*
> *strengthen collaboration as a strategy of change*
> *and educational improvement. (Ahumada-Figueroa*
> *et al., 2016, p. 13)*

Leading Downwards

Brown and Flood (2019) argue that to ensure and maximize the benefit of schools engaging in PLN, school leaders can perform three courses of action that help engage PLN activities in their schools: (1) formalize: keep staff on track, reminding and supporting PLN projects as priorities, ensuring that the work of the PLN is explicitly connected will school goals and outcomes; (2) prioritize: support and remind school staff that the PLN projects and activities are not additional tasks for the school, instead that they are part of their current functions, making sure that the staff is aware of the importance and potential impact of PLNs; and (3) mobilize: linking the PLN activities with their own school improvement plan, staff hours, school goals and strategies. In the words of the authors:

> *Key areas that are required if schools leaders are to*
> *maximise the impact to their schools of engaging*
> *in Professional Learning Networks (...) the need*
> *first formalise a school's and teachers' participation*
> *in the PLN to ensure that it remains a key focus of*
> *the school and that its importance is recognised.*
> *Second, school leaders also need to prioritise*

> *engagement to ensure adequate resources exist to allow the work of the PLN to get done. Finally, there is a need for school leaders to enable new knowledge and practices to be mobilized effectively to ensure there are adopted and employed thus ensuring their impact is maximized across the school as a whole. (Brown & Flood, 2019, p. 79)*

Formalizing, prioritizing and mobilizing can be understood as network leadership practices focusing on engaging schools and networks. For the purpose of this discussion, we define these practices as *leading downwards*, that is, from the network to the schools and from the schools to the network.

The idea of *leading downwards* has been a permanent, exiting and productive reflection among PLN scholars, especially to better understand and develop the role of *brokers* (Briscoe, Pollock, Campbell, & Carr-Harris, 2015; Brown & Flood, 2019; Brown & Poortman, 2018; Chitpin, 2014; Hubers & Poortman, 2018). For example, Poortman and Brown (2018) also describe activities that brokers can perform *leading downwards*: *identification, coordination and reflection* and *transformation*. *Identification* refers to detecting and signaling the differences between the new practices of networks and how they differ from their own community. *Coordination and reflection* involve understanding the underlying meaning of practices discussed in the PLN and to coordinate new routines in their own communities based on network knowledge. *Transformation* becomes visible when schools change and improve their existing practices related to PLN activities, which is central for school improvement. The mixed-methods analysis of the SIN strategy highlights that network members will benefit a great deal by developing these leadership practices to *lead downwards*.

Lateral Leadership

The evidence from the SIN strategy suggests that network members need to develop their capacity to work collectively among professional with different power positions. In our analysis, we conceptualize this capacity as *lateral leadership*. Three examples from the multi-site case study highlight the value of this type of network leadership (SINs 4, 5 and 13). In these cases, ministry supervisors were able to analyze key policy instruments with network members in a contextualized way, including the active voice of principals and curriculum coordinators. Also, in these SINs, network purposes were defined based on individual and collective performance self-evaluation or by a consultative process led by the ministry supervisor. To agree on a common purpose that is appropriate to the collective needs of partner schools, *lateral leadership* is very important because it requires involving different voices to define a goal valuable for all network members.

In these cases, participants declare that they shared meaningful practices within their networks, which entailed generating trustful and bidirectional relationships among network members. In the SIN scenario, considering a national policy, it seems relevant that a good brokering capacity is not possible if network does not also develop this lateral leadership. PLNs that seek to support knowledge creation and then mobilize that knowledge between networks and schools require a strong *lateral leadership* capacity. Supervisors' skills to develop relationship of trust with network participants, and among all network members, make a significant difference to allow networks to agree on implementing concrete collaborative projects that could support change and improvement efforts in partner schools.

Lateral leadership is also defined by the literature as distributed leadership. Harris (2014) argues that distributed leadership implies changes in the distribution of power, control and authority, thus distributed leadership must be understood from a micropolitical perspective. Recently, discussing the idea of network leadership, Azorín, Harris, and Jones (2019) highlight the relevance of distributed leadership as a key component of networking. This distributed perspective allows the development of leadership practices considering the expertise of network members, mobilizing knowledge within, between and across partners. The authors clearly state that "distributed leadership is mainly concerned with interactions rather than actions, with capacity building rather than control, with empowerment rather than coercion" (Azorín et al., 2019, p. 11).

Furthermore, a distributed perspective implies that leadership is not limited to a role or person (Harris & DeFlaminis, 2016; Spillane, Camburn, Pustejovsky, Stitziel Pareja, & Lewis, 2008), but it can be interchangeable between members, according to specific needs of the network. As a result, distributed leadership allows to focus the energy in developing the capacities and practices of network members, effectively generating rich horizontal relations among members, which could be very valuable for the sustainability of SINs and other types of PLNs (Azorín et al., 2019).

Another key aspect of distributed leadership is the possibility of dealing with power relationships among network members, allowing that the interest of the supervisor does not interfere with the capacity building of the network members. As we have previously discussed, there is a dark side to collaboration, involving negative dimensions of collaboration that are an important reminder that not all collaboration is successful, as the fabricated cooperation and contrived collegiality, where not everyone engages in collaborative activity with sound motives. The literature highlights that vertical centralized networks such as those where the agenda is contrived by those who occupy positions of power do not promote collaboration and might even incite resistance instead of professional learning (Greany & Ehren, 2016).

This idea is very relevant for mandated networks, such as SINs, which might have the intention of supporting network members in sharing practices and knowledge, but to achieve that goal, a shift in power relations should be evidenced in practice. One of the issues found in the mixed-methods analysis of the SIN strategy was that some networks were instrumental for the dissemination of ministry policies and information by supervisors, replicating the hierarchy of the Chilean education system within the network space. A national policy to support PLNs should be very careful about the position and role of the supervisor, and his or her capacity to facilitate horizontal relations among participants within the network space. In part, this requires to deeply reflect about their power position in order to foster networks as spaces of collective learning and inquiry, and avoid becoming spaces bureaucratized by the influence of national mandates.

Leading Upwards

Hatcher (2008) points out that school networks, such as PLNs, "offer the potential of new participatory relationships among teachers across schools, but also the potential of simply being vehicles for the transmission and implementation of government agendas" (p. 29). An explicit and well-developed distributed leadership within networks might help them evolve beyond an external mandate, and the evidence from the multi-site case study and national questionnaire tends to corroborate that it is possible for SINs to be much more than a governmental initiative. Nevertheless, distributed leadership does not guarantee that the national SIN strategy will be influenced by network members, especially within a market-oriented educational system that does not value collaboration for improvement and prefers competition for individual survival. Thus, the question about sustainability remains.

One way of addressing this challenge is by explicitly taking into consideration teachers' and leaders' moral purpose, and how this can prompt them to exert influence on people in decision-making positions. Boylan (2016) argues that this represents a professional identity

> *centered on professional learning, participation
> in school and teacher communities, collaboration
> with teachers and others, cooperative forms of
> professional development and organizational
> relationships and activism based on moral and
> social purposes. (p. 65)*

Such identity can rapidly flourish in a PLN environment, evolving into a systemic perspective about leadership, taking advantage of the network space to support collective actions aimed at the general improvement of education, which is a central component of systemic improvement.

A national educational policy that seeks to promote PLNs, to change a culture of individual competition for a more collaborative culture, should be explicit about the professional identity and moral purpose that such change requires. Also, the practices of those who lead that change should be constantly modeling what is expected. As Hargreaves and Fullan (2012) argue, to promote the change, school, district and governments have to *be the change*. SINs require to transform the power relationship among principals, curriculum coordinators, supervisor and local administration representatives. PLNs at a national scale will have to address the complex question of how to shift traditional power relationships, especially in challenging contexts. Consequently, we argue that network leaders need to lead downwards, laterally, but also need to *lead upwards*.

Leading upwards considers that a policy, such as the SIN should empower network members to be able to influence stakeholders in other levels of the educational system according to the purpose, actions and values of their network. In this sense, leading upwards is related to the idea of supporting *activist professionals* (Hargreaves, 2013) within networks, as a way of generating appropriate conditions to engage in collaboration and partnership in a given context. Consequently, leading upwards is a complex skill because it might entail weakening the position of power of those who are pushing forward the SIN strategy, in order to empower school leaders to exert ownership and perhaps transform the policy as it was originally conceived by policymakers. For instance, in the multi-site case study, participants were eager to involve different professional into the networks, not only principals and curriculum coordinators, as a way for networks to create meaningful relationships with other professionals who could be key agents of change in schools. Of course, this implies challenging the initial design of the SIN strategy that envisioned these networks, as spaces especially dedicated to the involvement of those who occupy formal leadership roles.

The notion of leading upwards is similar to Rincón-Gallardo's (2019) proposal about liberating learning, which states that sustainable improvement needs to find

> *ways to change the institutional logic of the system where they operate, leaving behind vertical relationship of authority and control over schools, and nurturing instead horizontal relationship of dialogue, co-learning, and mutual influence between the central leadership and the schools. (p. 31)*

In a challenging context, such as the market-oriented system in Chile, the three capacities of network leadership are crucial for the sustainability of PLN. Systemic leaders need to lead downwards to generate changes in schools, lead laterally from a distributed perspective to support and enhance strong ties among network members and lead upwards to influence key stakeholders in other levels of the educational system so that they can visualize the value of networks to promote the systemic improvement of education.

These systemic leadership practices echo Townsend (2015) argument about hybrid leadership, which is related to formal roles that professional occupy within an organizational structure or a network, and also leadership practices that emerge from the interests of network members, which is not necessarily associated with a formal role. These two types are usually in tension. On the one hand, there is a need for greater autonomy in decision making by agents of the network. On the other hand, there is a need to integrate and coordinate the different interests of network agents with the requirement of the system. Systemic leaders face the challenge to choose wisely which of those practices to apply considering the context of the network. Part of network learning is how bottom-up leadership can be exercised so that the local is considered in the design of the district's global infrastructure. Network leaders can play an important role in balancing these two properties within, between and beyond networks to co-design the system's infrastructure (Hopkins & Woulfin, 2015).

SYSTEM INFRASTRUCTURE

For the third element necessary to ensure the sustainability of SINs as professional learning networks in a challenging context, it is critical to think about the *system infrastructure* that would allow the articulation between the different levels of the system. This articulation should be based on a general agreement that education quality and equity is a shared responsibility of the system. Hopkins and Woulfin (2015) state that both top-down and bottom-up reforms are insufficient by themselves to generate a structure that facilitates change and school improvement. They propose a broader view to understand how the networks and system tools are related at their different levels (i.e., state, district, school and classroom). The concept of system infrastructure can be useful to understand how school leaders and teachers reformulate policies, tools and structures based on their leadership and teaching practices. However, it is important to consider how this structure can sustain or restrict educational change, and how much it can allow to sustain or transform practices.

Hopkins and Woulfin (2015) argue that the users of the system should be considered as designers since it is in the local practices where tools make sense and are (re)designed according to the context. The systemic approach can be useful to understand the collaboration between different sectors of education as well as changes in community-based educational reforms. Systemic improvement, from this perspective, involves considering that systemic leaders have a relevant role in the transformation of the system. The influence that these leaders may have in the design of the networking strategy and in their adaptation to the local context makes these leaders key agents for the transformation of the system. The sustainability of the networks depends not only on how well a network works but also on how this network supports a systemic improvement.

The system infrastructure necessary to provide sustainability to PLNs can also be considered from the perspective of the intermediate level: district, municipality or local administrator. At this level of the education system, different networks can coexist with different purposes and different agents. However, for an improvement strategy at this level to be successful, there must be an infrastructure that brings cohesion and coherence to this diversity of networks. Mobilizing knowledge implies not only connecting educational policies with what happens within school but also redesigning the policy at other levels in a way that is consistent with the reality of the local context.

The formalization of processes at the intermediate level involves considering the social and historical context of each network and the priorities that this level has set for PLNs throughout its territory. In the case of Chile, the work carried out by SINs toward schools and between schools must, therefore, be linked to the work planned by stakeholders at the intermediate level, ministry provincial departments and local administrators, understanding that PMEs at the school level must have coherence with policies and strategies at the intermediate level. The mobilization of knowledge in all these directions requires a strong system infrastructure that facilitates the coordination and articulation of different stakeholders as a way to achieve systemic improvement.

FOSTERING SYSTEMIC IMPROVEMENT IN CHALLENGING CONTEXTS

International evidence shows that numerous educational systems have opted for the strategy of networking to support improvement not only of those schools in difficulty but also the entire system as a whole (Feys & Devos, 2015; Rincón-Gallardo & Fullan, 2016). The idea behind this change is based on empirical evidence of how difficult it is for a school to improve on its own. School improvement from this new perspective assumes that efforts must be at all levels of the system, avoiding blaming a school for its success or failure. SINs seek to overcome the logic of individual accountability, promoting collaboration and co-responsibility between all levels of the system (González, Pino-Yancovic, & Ahumada-Figueroa, 2017). This change of logic implies a shift from a culture of individual accountability toward a culture of collaboration.

In Chile, according to Montecinos, Ahumada, Galdames, Campos, and Leiva (2015), principals are simultaneously subjected to accountability demands from three different sources: market (parental choice), state (quality assurance system based on standardized testing and school inspection) and from the municipal government that employs public school principals (employment contract with predefined performance targets). This focus on performativity is in line with the quasi-market educational model for the provision of educational services that have operated in Chile since 1980 and, with it, the imposition of a managerial approach to regulate principals' work priorities.

The consequence of this demand for accountability from different levels of the system is a distrust of the possible support that the system can offer. For Ryan (2005), the problem is not accountability per se, but the need for a more democratic one. Questions such as "for what" and "to whom" schools should be accountable are crucial for a market-oriented educational system (Montecinos et al., 2015). Anderson (2011), for example, has argued that school leaders and teachers need to be responsible for advancing a human rights agenda and education as a social right. The challenge seems to be how we go from an individual to collective accountability between all levels of the system and to start rethinking "for what" school leaders should be accountable for. A good path would be start shaping accountability for the democratic project, as Cochran-Smith et al. (2018) have argued for teacher education:

> *Instead of rejecting accountability in teacher education, then, we want to rescue it from the market quagmire and reclaim it for the democratic project. This is an exceedingly difficult task. To forward a democratic approach to accountability, we must find ways to define accountability's purposes and goals in terms of the common good, change the narrative about the problem of teacher education, and radically disrupt existing power relationship. All of this must happen in the context of an acutely polarized society wherein individualism and private goods have been valorized, and there are vast divides in people's deepest beliefs about the purposes of education, the challenges posed by diversity, and the meaning of equity, effectiveness, and national progress. (p. 153)*

In a market-driven educational oriented system, this new form of accountability seems extremely challenging, especially if schools are threatened to be closed if they do not achieve positive outcomes in a standardized test. SINs support alternative practical approaches to educational improvement that do not rely solely on individual performance and compliance of standards, focusing on the collective development of professional capital. The mixed-methods research presented in this book illustrates that this change is possible, as many networks are not only doing things better, more effectively, but they are also building new positive relationships among school leaders.

Principals and curriculum coordinators value the opportunity of sharing knowledge with others, and some of them provide concrete examples of how they use this knowledge to improve the educational quality of their schools. Consequently, SINs support the production of professional capital of its participants. Nevertheless, SINs require that school leaders and supervisors develop systemic leadership capacities in order to facilitate knowledge mobilization and the production of professional capital. There is also great diversity of network functioning, while some networks have been able to mobilize meaningful knowledge about collaborative practices, others have just been used as informative spaces to disseminate educational policies. The idea of promoting a culture of collaboration, shared responsibility and systemic improvement still requires to recognize and empower school leaders to influence the practices of others, and above all, to influence the structure of the educational system. PLNs will possibly be more sustainable not only because they can be able to support a different perspective of educational improvement but also because they can actually allow to restructure the entire educational system.

Table 3. Percentage of Agreement by Item in Networking Dimension.

Item	Totally Disagree (%)	Disagree (%)	Somewhat Disagree (%)	Somewhat Agree (%)	Agree (%)	Totally Agree (%)	Not Applicable (%)
In my network, we evaluate how our work contributes to our schools' improvement.	2.7	4.9	5.9	18.4	40.8	25.9	1.3
In my network, there are norms for dealing with conflict that arise as a result of differences in opinions.	2.6	5.2	5.1	16.6	37.9	21.5	11.1
My network contributes to solve problems at our own schools.	2.3	3.6	6.4	20.2	42.0	24.2	1.3
In my network, we have created new knowledge by searching for solutions to shared issues.	2.5	3.5	5.1	18.6	43.9	25.0	1.4
My network established mechanisms and communications channels to link up with community actors and institutions.	2.8	9.2	7.4	24.1	34.8	17.0	4.7
In my network, we have shared responsibilities among its members.	1.8	2.8	4.6	16.5	43.9	29.0	1.3

(Continued)

Table 3. (*Continued*)

Item	Totally Disagree (%)	Disagree (%)	Somewhat Disagree (%)	Somewhat Agree (%)	Agree (%)	Totally Agree (%)	Not Applicable (%)
In my network, there are leaders who help resolve differences in opinion and internal conflicts.	2.0	2.8	3.2	16.6	41.1	24.9	9.5
My network facilitates the development of skills and professional development of its members.	2.1	3.1	5.5	17.5	44.4	26.5	0.9
My network's agenda is developed based on the priorities and interests expressed by its participants.	3.4	4.9	5.8	16.2	37.2	31.1	1.3
The members of my network participate actively in the planned activities.	1.8	2.8	4.3	19.0	45.4	26.1	0.8
Being in the network fosters a shared view for defining our network needs.	1.9	2.4	3.5	14.8	42.1	34.2	0.9
My interest to participate in network meetings has increased since the first meeting.	3.3	5.0	5.6	16.1	37.6	31.4	1.0
The members of my network share their schools' practice to achieve our network objectives.	1.5	2.3	2.8	14.2	43.0	35.1	1.2

Table 4. Percentage of Agreement by Item in Professional Capital Dimension.

Item	Totally Disagree (%)	Disagree (%)	Somewhat Disagree (%)	Somewhat Agree (%)	Agree (%)	Totally Agree (%)	Not Applicable (%)
In my network, I feel I participate at the same level as other members.	1.7	1.6	2.1	9.4	40.4	44.1	0.7
In my network, the opinions of principals and curriculum coordinators are equally respected than those of general members.	1.9	1.3	1.8	7.9	37.1	49.1	1.0
In my network, I feel there is trust to freely express my perceptions and disagreements.	2.0	1.8	2.8	10.4	37.9	44.5	0.7
The decisions made in my network are agreed among its members.	2.1	2.2	3.3	11.5	40.9	39.0	1.1
The tasks in my network are carried out by teams including professionals from across all participating schools.	2.4	3.6	4.3	13.5	40.3	33.9	1.7

(Continued)

Table 4. (Continued)

Item	Totally Disagree (%)	Disagree (%)	Somewhat Disagree (%)	Somewhat Agree (%)	Agree (%)	Totally Agree (%)	Not Applicable (%)
In my network, there are spaces of trust and mutual understanding among members.	1.8	1.8	3.9	14.6	41.6	35.1	1.2
My network favors cooperation among its members.	1.7	2.1	3.1	12.9	42.1	37.5	0.7
I participate in the decision-making process of my network.	2.2	3.8	3.5	17.6	40.5	30.4	2.1
School networks contribute to share resources among participant schools.	1.6	1.2	2.5	12.4	38.8	42.6	0.9

Table 5. Percentage of Agreement by Item in Network for Improvement Dimension.

Items	Totally Disagree (%)	Disagree (%)	Somewhat Disagree (%)	Somewhat Agree (%)	Agree (%)	Totally Agree (%)	Not Applicable (%)
Participating in the network has improved my leadership skills.	3.0	5.2	4.5	22.2	39.6	23.0	2.3
My network helps me find solutions to problems that I face in my school.	2.4	4.4	5.3	20.1	40.2	26.7	0.8
The members of my network understand that the work done is fundamental to improve school management.	2.2	3.1	3.8	15.9	40.0	33.8	1.1
I feel very committed to the work we do in my school improvement network.	2.3	2.9	2.7	11.8	40.1	39.5	0.7
The actions of my network are organized to address students' educational needs.	2.5	3.7	4.0	19.0	38.2	31.6	0.9
The ideas that arise from my network have been implemented as actions or projects in my school.	2.6	3.8	4.2	22.0	44.5	21.5	1.4

(Continued)

Table 5. *(Continued)*

Items	Totally Disagree (%)	Disagree (%)	Somewhat Disagree (%)	Somewhat Agree (%)	Agree (%)	Totally Agree (%)	Not Applicable (%)
The participation of the members of my network contributes to the work done in my school.	2.3	3.1	3.8	20.6	44.7	24.2	1.3
I use the knowledge generated in my network in my school.	2.2	2.0	1.7	12.7	42.7	38.0	0.8
My network promotes that all members are creators of new ideas or projects.	3.6	4.6	3.0	15.6	41.1	31.1	1.0
The topics discussed in my network are appropriate to the school context where I work.	1.6	2.3	2.3	10.4	40.6	42.5	0.5

REFERENCES

Ahumada-Figueroa, L., González, A., Pino, M., & Galdames, S. (2016). *Marco para el Liderazgo Sistémico y el Aprendizaje en Red: Los Desafíos de la Colaboración en Contextos de Competencia* [Framwork for Systemic Leadership and Network Learning: The Challenges of Collaboration in Competitive Contexts]. Informe Técnico No. 2. LIDERES EDUCATIVOS, Centro de Liderazgo para la Mejora Escolar: Chile.

Ahumada, L., González, A., & Pino, M. (2016). *Redes de Mejoramiento Escolar: ¿Por qué son importantes y cómo las apoyamos?* [School improvement networks: Why are they important and how do we support them?] Documento de Trabajo No. 1. Líderes Educativos, Centro de Liderazgo para la Mejora Escolar, Chile.

Ahumada, L., Montecinos, C., & González, A. (2012). Quality assurance in Chile's municipal schools: Facing the challenge of assuring and improving quality in low performing schools. In M. Savsar (Ed.), *Quality assurance and management* (pp. 183–192). Rijeka, Croatia: InTech.

Ainscow, M. (2016). *Struggles for equity in education*. London: Routledge.

Ainscow, M., Dyson, A., Goldrick, A., & West, M. (2016). Using collaborative inquiry to foster equity within school systems: Opportunities and barriers. *School Effectiveness and School Improvement, 27*(1), 7–23. doi:10.1080/092434 53.2014.939591

Ainscow, M., & West, M. (Eds.). (2006). *Improving urban schools: Leadership and collaboration.* Maidenhead: Open University Press.

Anderson, G., & Herr, K. (2007). El docente-investigador: Investigación – Acción como una forma válida de generación de conocimientos. [Teacher research: Action research as a valid form of knowledge generation.] In I. Sverdlick (Ed.), *La investigacion educativa: Una herramienta de conocimiento y de accion.* Buenos Aires: Noveduc.

Apple, M. W. (2005). Education, markets, and an audit culture. *Critical Quarterly, 47,* 11–29. doi:10.1111/j.0011-1562.2005.00611.x.

Armstrong, P. W., & Ainscow, M. (2018). School-to-school support within a competitive education system: Views from the inside. *School Effectiveness and School Improvement, 29*(4), 614–633.

Avalos, B. (1999). *Desarrollo docente en el contexto de la institución escolar. Los microcentros rurales y los grupos profesionales de trabajo en Chile* [Teacher development in the school context . Rural microcenters and professional groups in Chile]. Material de apoyo para la Conferencia "Los Maestros en América Latina: Nuevas Perspectivas sobre su Desarrollo y Desempeño." San José, Costa Rica (pp. 28–30).

Azorín, C. M., & Muijs, D. (2017). Networks and collaboration in Spanish education policy. *Educational Research, 59*(3), 273–296.

Azorín, C., Harris, A., & Jones, M. (2019). Taking a distributed perspective on leading professional learning networks. *School Leadership and Management,* 1–17. doi:10.1080/13632434.2019.1647418

Bellei, C. (2015). *El gran experimento* [The great experiment]. Santiago, Chile: LOM Ediciones.

Bellei, C. (2018). *La Nueva Educación Pública. Contexto, contenidos y perspectivas de la desmunicipalización* [The New Public Education: Contexts, contents and perspectives about the desmunicipalization]. Santiago, Chile: CIAE.

Bellei, C., & Cabalín, C. (2013). Chilean student movements: Sustained struggle to transform a market oriented educational system. *Current Issues in Comparative Education*, *15*(2), 108–123.

Bellei, C., & Vanni, X. (2015). The evolution of educational policy in Chile 1980–2014. In S. Schwartzman (Ed.), *Education in South America*. London: Bloomsburry Publishing.

Boylan, M. (2016). Deepening system leadership: Teachers leading from below. *Educational Management Administration and Leadership*, *44*(1), 57–72.

Briscoe, P., Pollock, K., Campbell, C., & Carr-Harris, S. (2015). Finding the sweet spot: Network structures and processes for increased knowledge mobilization. *Brock Education: A Journal of Educational Research and Practice*, *25*(1), 19–34.

Brown, C., & Flood. J. (2019). *Formalise, prioritise and mobilise: How school leaders secure the benefits of professional learning networks*. Bingley: Emerald Publishing.

Brown, C., & Poortman, C. L. (Eds.). (2018). *Networks for learning: Effective collaboration for teacher, school and system improvement*. London: Routledge.

Bryk, A. S., Gomez, L. M., & Grunow, A. (2010). *Getting ideas into action: Building networked improvement communities in education*. Carnegie Foundation for the Advancement of Teaching. Stanford, CA.

Bryk, A. S., Gomez, L. M., Grunow, A., & LeMahieu, P. G. (2015). *Learning to improve: How America's schools can get better at getting better*. Boston, MA: Harvard University Press.

Cáceres, P. (2003). Análisis cualitativo de contenido: Una alternativa metodológica alcanzable [Qualitative content analysis: One achievable methodological alternative]. *Psicoperspectivas*, 2, 53–82.

Campbell, C. (2018). Realizing professional capital by, for, and with the learning profession: Lessons from Canada. In H. J. Malone, S. Rincón-Gallardo, & K. Kew (Eds.), *Future directions of educational change: Social justice, professional capital, and systems change* (pp. 117–134). New York, NY: Routledge. Retrieved from http://www.routledge.com/Future-Directions-of-Educational-Change-Social-Justice-Professional-Capital/Malone-Rincon-Gallardo-Kew/p/book/9781138283916

Campbell, C., Osmond-Johnson, P., Sohn, J., & Lieberman, A. (2017). Teacher policies and practices in Ontario. In C. Campbell, K. Zeichner, A. Lieberman, & P. Osmond-Johnson, with J. Hollar, S. Pisani, & J. Sohn (Eds.), *Empowered educators in Canada: How high-performing systems shape teacher quality* (pp. 87–196). San Francisco, CA: Jossey-Bass.

Carpenter, D. (2017). Collaborative inquiry and the shared workspace of professional learning communities. *International Journal of Educational Management*, 21(1), 17–28.

Carrasco, A., & Fromm, G. (2016). How local market pressures shape leadership practices: Evidence from Chile. *Journal of Educational Administration and History*, 48(4), 290–308.

Chapman, C. (2013). Academy federations, chains and teaching schools in England: Reflections on leadership, policy and practice. *Journal of School Choice: International Research and Reform*, 7(3), 334–352. doi:10.1080/15582159.2013.808936

Chapman, C. (2015). From one school to many: Reflections on the impact and nature of school federations and chains in England. *Educational Management Administration and Leadership*, 43(1), 46–60. Retrieved from https://doi.org/10.1177/1741143213494883

Chapman, C. (2019). From hierarchies to networks. *Journal of Educational Administration*, 57(5), 554–570.

Chapman, C., Chestnutt, H., Friel, N., Hall, S., & Lowden, K. (2016a). Professional capital and collaborative inquiry networks for educational equity and improvement? *Journal of Professional Capital and Community*, 1(3), 178–197.

Chapman, C., Lowden, K., Chestnutt, H., Hall, S., McKinney, S., & Friel, N. (2016b). *The school improvement partnership programme: Sustaining collaboration and inquiry to tackle educational inequity*. Project Report. Education Scotland, Livingston, Scotland.

Chapman, C., Lowden, K., Chestnutt, H., Hall, S., McKinney, S., & Hulme, M. (2014). *Research on the impact of the school improvement partnership programme*. Interim Report. Education Scotland, Livingston, Scotland.

Chapman, C., Lowden, K., Chestnutt, H. R., Hall, S., McKinney, S., Hulme, M., & Friel, N. (2015). *The school improvement partnership programme: Using collaboration and inquiry to tackle educational inequity*. Livingston: Education Scotland.

Chapman, C., & Muijs, D. (2013). Does school-to-school collaboration promote school improvement? A study of the impact of school federations on student outcomes. *School Effectiveness and School Improvement*, *25*(3), 351–393. Retrieved from https://doi.org/10.1080/09243453.2013.840319

Chitpin, S. (2014). Principals and the professional learning community: Learning to mobilize knowledge. *International Journal of Educational Management*, *28*(2), 215–229. https://doi.org/10.1108/IJEM-04-2013-0044

Cochran-Smith, M., Cummings Carney, M., Stringer Keefe, E., Burton, B., Chang, W., Fernández, M. B., ... Baker, M. (2018). *Reclaiming accountability in teacher education.* New York, NY: Teachers College Press.

Creswell, J. (2008). *Research design: Qualitative, quantitative, and mixed methods approaches.* Los Angeles, CA: Sage.

Creswell, J. (2011). *Controversies in mixed methods research.* In N. Denzin & Y. Lincoln (Eds.), *The Sage handbook of qualitative research* (pp. 269–317). Thousand Oaks, CA: Sage.

DeLuca, C., Shulha, J., Luhanga, U., Shulha, L., Christou, T., & Klinger, D. (2015). Collaborative inquiry as a professional learning structure for educators: A scoping review. *Professional Development in Education*, *41*(4), 640–670. doi:10.1080/19415257.2014.933120

DEP. (2018). *Estudio diagnóstico de las variables asociadas a las condiciones para la conformación de redes de establecimientos educacionales, en los primeros cuatro Servicios Locales de Educación Pública* [Diagnostic study of the variables associated with the conditions for the formation of networks of schools, in the first four Local Services of Public Education]. Santiago, Chile: Dirección de Educación Pública.

Díaz-Gibson, J., Civís-Zaragoza, M., & Guàrdia-Olmos, J. (2014). Strengthening education through collaborative networks: Leading the cultural change. *School Leadership and Management, 34*(2), 179–200.

Duffy, G., & Gallagher, T. (2017). Shared education in contested spaces: How collaborative networks improve communities and schools. *Journal of Educational Change, i*(1), 107–134.

Ehren, M., & Perryman, J. (2018). Accountability of school networks: Who is accountable to whom and for what? *Educational Management Administration and Leadership, 46*(6), 942–959.

Elliott, J. (1991). *Action research for educational change.* Milton Keynes: Open University Press.

Falabella, A. (2016). Do national test scores and quality labels trigger school self-assessment and accountability? A critical analysis in the Chilean context. *British Journal of Sociology of Education, 37*(5), 743–760.

Feys, E., & Devos, G. (2015). What comes out of incentivized collaboration: A qualitative analysis of eight flemish school networks. *Educational Management Administration & Leadership, 43*(5), 738.

Fuentealba, R., & Galaz, A. (2008). La reflexión como recurso para la mejora de las practices docentes en servicio: El caso de las Redes Pedagógicas Locales [Reflection as a resource for the improvement of teaching practices in service: The case of Local Pedagogical Networks]. In J. Cornejo & R. Fuentealba (Eds.), *Prácticas reflexivas para la formación profesional docente ¿qué las hace eficaces? [Reflective practices for teachers professional development,*

what makes them effective?] (pp. 141–168). Santiago:
Ediciones UCSH.

González, A., Pino-Yancovic, M., & Ahumada-Figueroa,
L. (2017). *Transitar desde el mejoramiento escolar al
mejoramiento sistémico: Oportunidades y desafíos de
las redes escolares en Chile* [Transiting from school
improvement to systemic improvement: Opportunities and
challenges for school networks in Chile]. Nota Técnica
No. 2-2017, LIDERES EDUCATIVOS, Centro de Liderazgo
para la Mejora Escolar, Pontificia Universidad Católica de
Valparaíso, Valparaíso, Chile.

González-Weil, C., Cortéz, M., Pérez, J., Bravo, P., &
Ibaceta, Y. (2013). Construyendo dominios de encuentro
para problematizar acerca de las prácticas pedagógicas de
profesores secundarios de Ciencias: Incorporando el modelo
de Investigación-Acción como plan de formación continua
[Building encounter domains to problematize secondary
science teachers' practice: Incorporating the action-research
model as a continuous development plan]. *Estudios
Pedagógicos, 39*(2), 129–146.

Greany, T., & Ehren, M. C. M. (2016). Written evidence
to Education Select Committee inquiry into the
performance, accountability and governance of Multi-
Academy Trusts. Retrieved from http://data.parliament.uk/
writtenevidence/committeeevidence.svc/evidencedocument/
educationcommittee/multiacademy-trusts/written/32050.html

Greene, J. (2006). Evaluation, democracy, and social change.
In I. Shaw, I. G. R. Shaw, J. C. Greene, & M. M. Mark
(Eds.), *The Sage handbook of evaluation*. London: Sage.

Greene, J. C. (2007). *Mixed methods in social inquiry*.
San Francisco, CA: Jossey-Bass.

Hadfield, M., & Chapman, C. (2009). *Leading school-based networks*. London: Routledge.

Hargreaves, A. (1994). *Changing teachers, changing times teachers' work and culture in the postmodern age*. London: Cassell.

Hargreaves, A., & Fullan, M. (2012). *Professional capital: Transforming teaching in every school*. New York, NY: Teachers College Press.

Harris, A. (2014). *Distributed leadership matters: Perspectives, practicalities, and potential*. Thousand Oaks, CA: Corwin.

Harris, A., & DeFlaminis, J. (2016). Distributed leadership in practice: Evidence, misconceptions and possibilities. *Management in Education, 30*(4), 141–146.

Harvey, D. (2007). *Breve historia del neoliberalismo [A Brief History of Neoliberalism]*. Madrid, España: Akal.

Hatcher, R. (2008). System leadership, networks and the question of power. *Management in Education, 22*(2), 24–30.

Holmlund, T., Deuel, A., Slavit, D., & Kennedy, A. (2010). Leading deep conversations in collaborative inquiry groups. *The Clearing House: A Journal of Educational Strategies, Issues and Ideas, 83*(5), 175–179.

Hopkins, D., Ainscow, M., & West, M. (1994). *School improvement in an era of change*. London: Cassell.

Hopkins, M., & Woulfin, S. L. (2015). School system (re)design: Developing educational infrastructures to support school leadership and teaching practice. *Journal of Educational Change, 16*(4), 371–377. doi:10.1007/s10833-015-9260-6

Hubers, M. D., & Poortman, C. L. (2018). Establishing sustainable school improvement through Professional Learning Networks. In *Networks for learning: Effective collaboration for teacher, school and system improvement*. London: Routledge Taylor and Francis Group.

Jackson, D., & Temperley, J. (2006). From professional learning community to networked learning community. Paper presented at the *International Congress for School Effectiveness and Improvement (ICSEI)*, January 3–6, Fort Lauderdale.

Jeong, D. W., & Luschei, T. F. (2018). Are teachers losing control of the classroom? Global changes in school governance and teacher responsibilities, 2000–2015. *International Journal of Educational Development*, 62, 289–301.

Johnson, R., & Gray, B. (2010). A history of philosophical and theoretical issues for mixed methods research. In A. Tashakkori & C. Teddlie (Eds.), *Sage handbook of mixed methods research* (2nd ed., pp. 69–94). Thousand Oaks, CA: Sage.

Katz, S., & Earl, L. (2010). Learning about networked learning communities. *School Effectiveness and School Improvement*, 21(1), 27–51. https://doi.org/10.1080/09243450903569718

Leithwood, K. (2018). Characteristics of effective leadership networks: A replication and extension. *School Leadership and Management*, 39(2), 1364–2626.

Leithwood, K., & Azah, V. N. (2016). Characteristics of effective leadership networks. *Journal of Educational Administration*, 54(4), 409–433. https://doi.org/10.1108/JEA-08-2015-0068

Lewin, K. (1946). Action research and minority problems. *Journal of Social Issues*, 2(4), 34–46. http://dx.doi.org/10.1111/j.1540-4560.1946.tb02295.x

Lieberman, A., & Grolnick, M. (1996). Networks and reform in American education. *Teacher College Record, 98*(1), 7–45.

Lipman, P. (2011). *The new political economy of urban education: Neoliberalism, race, and the right to the city.* New York, NY: Routledge.

Little, J. W. (1993). Teachers' professional development in a climate of educational reform. *Educational Evaluation and Policy Analysis, 15*(2), 129–151.

Lubienski, C. A., & Lubienski, S. T. (2014). *The public school advantage: Why public schools outperform private schools.* Chicago, IL: The University of Chicago Press.

Matthews, P., Moorman, H., & Nusche, D. (2008). Building a leadership capacity for system improvement in Victoria, Australia. *Improving School Leadership, 2,* 179–213.

Mayne, J., & Rieper, O. (2003). Collaborating for public service quality: The implications for evaluation. In A. Gray, B. Jenkins, F. Leeuw, & J. Mayne (Eds.), *Collaboration in public services: The challenge for evaluation* (pp. 105–131). New Brunswick, NJ: Transaction Publishers.

McCarthy, C., Pitton, V., Kim, S., & Monje, D. (2009). Movement and stasis in the neoliberal reorientation to schooling. In M. Apple, A. Wayne & L. Gandin (Eds.), *The Routledge international handbook of critical education* (pp. 36–50). London: Routledge.

McCarthy, C., & Sanya, B. N. (2014). The new iconography of the global city: Displacement and the residues of culture in Chicago. *Policy Futures in Education, 12*(8), 981–991. https://doi.org/10.2304/pfie.2014.12.8.981

McGinn, N., & Welsh, T. (1999). Decentralization of Education: Why, when, what and how? In W. D. Haddad &

T. Demsky (Eds.), *Fundamentals of educational planning*. París: Unesco-International Institute for Educational Planning.

Mifsud, D. (2016). The policy discourse of networking and its effect on school autonomy: A Foucauldian interpretation. *Journal of Educational Administration and History*, *48*(1), 89–112. https://doi.org/10.1080/00220620.2016.1092427

MINEDUC. (2016a). *Orientaciones para el apoyo técnico-pedagógico al sistema escolar [Guidance for pedagogical technical support to the school system]*. Santiago, Chile: División de Educación General.

MINEDUC. (2016b). *Términos de referencia: Estudio sobre la implementación de las redes de mejoramiento escolar [Term of references: Study on the implementation of school improvement networks]*. Santiago, Chile: División de Educación General, Ministerio de Educación de Chile.

MINEDUC. (2017a). *Estudio sobre la implementación de las Redes de Mejoramiento Escolar [Study on the implementation of school improvement networks]*. Chile: Ministerio de Educación.

MINEDUC. (2017b). *Plan de mejoramiento educativo 2017 [School Improvement plan 2017]*. Santiago, Chile: División de Educación General.

Mizala, A., & Romaguera, P. (2002). Evaluacion del desempeño e incentivos en la educacion chilena [Evaluation of the preformance and incentives of the Chilean education]. *Cuadernos de Economía*, *39*(118), 353–394. https://dx.doi.org/10.4067/S0717-68212002011800004

Montecinos, C., Ahumada, L., Galdames, S., Campos, F., & Leiva, M. V. (2015). Targets, threats and (dis)trust: The managerial troika for public school principals in Chile.

Education Policy Analysis Archives, *23*(87), 1–29.
doi:10.14507/epaa.v23.2083

Montecinos, C., Pino, M., Campos, J., Domínguez, R., &
Carreño, C. (2014). Master teachers as professional
developers: Managing conflicting versions of
professionalism. *Educational Management, Administration
and Leadership*, *42*(2), 275–292. http://dx.doi.org/10.1177/
1741143213502191

Moreno, C. (2007). Las escuelas rurales en Chile: La
municipalización y sus fortalezas y debilidades [Rural
schools in Chile: The municipalitzation, its strengths and its
weaknesses]. *Revista Digital eRural, Educación cultura y
desarrollo rural*, *4*(8), 1–6.

Muijs, D. (2010). Changing classroom learning.
In A. Hargreaves, A. Lieberman, M. Fullan, & D. Hopkins
(Eds.), *Second international handbook of educational change*
(Vol. 23, pp. 237–258). New York, NY: Springer International
Handbooks of Education. doi:10.1007/978-90-481-2660-6_14

Muijs, D., West, M., & Ainscow, M. (2010). Why network?
Theoretical perspectives on networking. *School Effectiveness
and School Improvement*, *21*(1), 5–26.

Munby, S., & Fullan, M. (2016). Inside-out and downside-
up: How leading from the middle has the power to
transform education systems. Education Development
Trust. Retrieved from http://michaelfullan.ca/wp-content/
uploads/2016/02/Global-Dialogue-Thinkpiece

Noffke, S. (1995). Action research and democratic
schooling: Problematics and potentials. In S. Noffke &
R. B. Stevenson (Eds.), *Educational action research:
Becoming practically critical* (pp. 1–10). New York, NY:
Teachers College Press.

Núñez, C. G., Solís, C., & Soto, R. (2013). ¿Qué sucede en las comunidades cuando se cierra la escuela rural? Un análisis psicosocial de la política de cierre de las escuelas rurales en Chile [What happens in rural communities when school is closed? A psychosocial analysis about policy of closing rural schools in Chile]. *Universitas Psychologica, 13*(2), 651–625.

OECD. (2004). *Revisión de políticas nacionales en educación: Chile* [Reviews of National Policies for Education: Chile]. París, France and Santiago, Chile: MINEDUC.

Peirano, C., & Vargas, J. (2005). Private schools with public financing in Chile. In L. Wolff, J. C. Navarro, & P. González (Eds.), *Private education and public policy in Latin America* (pp. 7–38). Washington, DC: PREAL.

Peter-Koop, A., Santos-Wagner, V., Breen, C. J., & Begg, A. J. C. (Eds.). (2013). *Collaboration in teacher education: Examples from the context of mathematics education* (Vol. 1). Berlin, Germany: Springer Science & Business Media.

Pino, M., González, A., & Ahumada, L. (2018). *Indagación colaborativa: Elementos teóricos y prácticos para su uso en redes educativas [Collaborative inquiry: Theoretical and practical guidelines for the use in educational networks].* Informe Técnico No. 4. LIDERES EDUCATIVOS, Centro de Liderazgo para la Mejora Escolar, Valparaíso, Chile.

Pino-Yancovic, M. (2015). Parents' defense of their children's right to education: Resistance experiences against public school closings in Chile. *Education, Citizenship and Social Justice, 10*(3), 254–265.

Pino-Yancovic, M., Ahumda, L., Guzmán, J., Luna, D., Torres, N., & Valenzuela, J. P. (2019). Building networks and building trust supporting collaborative enquiry projects in challenging contexts. *International Congress for School Effectiveness and Improvement (ICSEI)*, Stavanger, Norway.

Pino-Yancovic, M., Oyarzún-Vargas, G., & Salinas-Barrios, I. (2016). Crítica a la rendición de cuentas: Narrativa de resistencia al sistema de evaluación en Chile [A critique to the standardization for accountability: narrative of resistance of the assessment system in Chile]. *Cadernos Cedes, 36*(100), 337–354

Poortman, C. L., & Brown, C. (2018). The importance of professional learning networks. In C. Brown & C. L. Poortman (Eds.), *Networks for learning* (pp. 32–41). London: Routledge.

Reason, P., & Bradbury, H. (2001). Inquiry and participation in search of a world worthy of human aspiration. In P. Reason & H. Bradbury (Eds.), *Handbook of action research: Participative inquiry and practice* (pp. 1–14). London: Sage.

Reid, S. (2014). Knowledge influencers: Leaders influencing knowledge creation and mobilization. *Journal of Educational Administration, 52*(3), 332–357. https://doi.org/10.1108/JEA-01-2013-0013

Rincón-Gallardo, S. (2019). *Liberating learning: Educational change as social movement.* New York, NY: Routledge.

Rincón-Gallardo, S., & Fullan, M. (2016). Essential features of effective networks in education. *Journal of Professional Capital and Community, 1*(1), 5–22. Retrieved from https://doi.org/10.1108/JPCC-09-2015-0007

Rizvi, F., & Lingard, B. (2010). *Globalizing education.* London: Routledge.

Robinson, V. M. (2008). Forging the links between distributed leadership and educational outcomes. *Journal of Educational Administration, 46*(2), 241–256.

Román, M. (2008). Focalización en educación: Límites y tensiones de una política que ha buscado mejorar la calidad y equidad del sistema educativo chileno [Focus on education: Limits and tensions of a policy that has sought to improve the quality and equity of the Chilean education system]. *Docencia, 35*, 4–16.

Ryan, K. (2005). Making educational accountability more democratic. *American Journal of Evaluation, 26*, 532–543. http://dx.doi.org/10.1177/1098214005281344

Schildkamp, K., Poortman, C. L., & Handelzalts, A. (2016). Data teams for school improvement. *School Effectiveness and School Improvement, 27*(2), 228–254.

Schön, D. (1984). *The reflective practitioner: How professionals think in action.* New York, NY: Basic Books.

Schwandt, T. (2000). Three epistemological stances for qualitative inquiry: Interpretivism, hermeneutics, and social constructionism. In *Handbook of qualitative research.* Retrieved from http://www.mao52115.tcu.edu.tw/handout/qr/04_Three Epistemological.pdf

Segone, M. (2011). *Evaluation for equitable development results.* New York, NY: UNICEF.

Shirley, D. (2016). Three forms of professional capital: Systemic, social movement, and activist. *Journal of Professional Capital and Community, 1*(4), 302–320. doi:10.1108/JPCC-08-2016-0020

Spillane, J. P., Camburn, E. M., Pustejovsky, J., Stitziel Pareja, A., & Lewis, G. (2008). Taking a distributed perspective. *Journal of Educational Administration, 46*(2), 189–213.

Stake, R. E. (2005). *Multiple case study analysis.* New York, NY: Guilford Press.

Stenhouse, L. (1975). *An Introduction to curriculum research and development.* London: Heinemann Educational.

Stoll, L., Bolam, R., McMahon, A., Wallace, M., & Thomas, S. (2006). Professional learning communities: A review of the literature. *Journal of Educational Change, 7*(4), 221–258.

Stoll, L., Moorman, H., & Rahm, S. (2008). Building leadership capacity for system improvement in Austria. *Improving School Leadership, 2,* 215–251.

Tarsilla, M. (2010). Conversation with Jennifer Greene. *Theorists' Theories of Evaluation, 6*(13), 209–219.

Taylor, M. (2006). *From Pinochet to the "Third Way": Neoliberalism and social transformation in Chile.* London: Pluto Press.

Teddlie, C. & Tashakkori, A. (2010). Overview of contemporary issues in mixed methods research. In A. Tashakkori & C. Teddlie (Eds.), *Handbook of mixed methods in social and behavioral research* (pp. 1–41). Thousand Oaks, CA: Sage.

Teddlie, C. & Tashakkori, A. (2011). Mixed methdos research: Contemporary issues in an emerging field. In N. Denzin & Y. Lincoln (Eds.), *The sage handbook of qualitative research.* (pp. 285–300). Thousand Oaks, CA: Sage.

Tejedor, F. J. (2012). Evaluación del desempeño docente [Teacher preformance evaluation]. *Revista Iberoamericana de Evaluación Educativa, 5*(1), 318–327.

Townsend, A. (2015). Leading school networks: Hybrid leadership in action? *Educational Management Administration and Leadership*, 43(5), 719–737.

Valenzuela, J., & Montecinos, C. (2017, July 27). Structural Reforms and Equity in Chilean Schools. Oxford Research Encyclopedia of Education. Retrieved from https://oxfordre.com/education/view/10.1093/acrefore/9780190264093.001.0001/acrefore-9780190264093-e-108. Accessed on September 25, 2019.

Valenzuela, J. P., Bellei, C., & De los Ríos, D. (2014). Socio-economic school segregation in a market oriented educational system. The case of Chile. *Journal of Education Policy*, 29(2), 217–241.

Verger, A., BonaL, X., & Zancajo, A. (2016). What are the role and impact of public–private partnerships in education? A realist evaluation of the Chilean education quasi-market. *Comparative Education Review*, 60(2), 223–248.

Warren-Little, J. (1990). The persistence of privacy: Autonomy and initiative in teachers' professional relations. *Teachers College Record*, 91(4), 509–535.

Wohlstetter, P., Malloy, C. L., Chau, D., & Polhemus, J. L. (2003). Improving schools through networks: A new approach to urban school reform. *Educational Policy*, 17(4), 399–430.

Zoro, B., Améstica, J., & Berkowitz, D. (2017). *Diagnosticografía: Aportes para la realización de diagnósticos territoriales desde el nivel intermedio* [Diagnosticography: Contributions for the realization of territorial diagnoses from the intermediate level]. Nota Técnica No. 10-2017, LIDERES EDUCATIVOS, Centro de Liderazgo para la Mejora Escolar, Chile.

Zoro, B., Berkowitz, D., Uribe, M., & Osorio, A. (2017). *Desafíos para la transformación del nivel intermedio en educación [Challenges for the transformation of the intermediate level into education]*. Informe Técnico No. 8 LIDERES EDUCATIVOS, Centro de Liderazgo para la Mejora Escolar, Chile.

INDEX